Praise for
Sales Professional's Guide to Writing Winning Proposals

When it comes to sales proposals that really close business, we've had it all backwards—for years! In his new book, Bob Kantin sets us straight. And it proves out in action. If you want to see a measurable difference in closing business when your proposal counts—and it counts more and more in today's complex selling world—pick up this book, read it, and keep it handy.

Bill Byron Concevitch
Chief Learning Officer, Verint
Author of *Counter-Intuitive Selling: Mastering the Art of the Unexpected*

If you sell in an industry that dictates the use of proposals, you need to read this book and put Bob's teachings into practice. The amazing thing about it is that it clearly defines what you need to do for every element of the proposal regardless of how short, long, or deep you need the document to be. The best thing you can do is make sure that your competition doesn't read it first!

Michael Norton, President
Zig Ziglar Corporation

A critical factor to closing more business is writing buyer-focused sales proposals. This book shows you how to do that and much more! Follow Bob Kantin's recommended structure if you want your proposals to become the benchmarks your prospects use to evaluate the competition—you'll win every time.

A key element of our success is the quality and consistency afforded by our automated proposal development process. This book is a must read if you are considering automation. It will help you understand how to integrate all the required processes and tools.

Kerry Barlow, Vice President, West Region
Securitas Security Systems

Bob Kantin proves, once again, that he is a thought leader in the art and science of business development. He offers practical advice and some new challenges in this must read book. We have used Bob's prior books in our training classes and will use this in our upcoming programs.

Troy Waugh, CPA, CEO
FiveStar3, LLC

The Rainmaker Academy... Rainmaker Consulting Group... Enterprise Network Worldwide

Michael Jordan has a philosophy that can help Johnny close more business, "I've always believed that if you put in the work, the results will come. I don't do things halfheartedly. Because I know if I do, then I can expect halfhearted results." Don't write sales proposals halfheartedly. Get practical tips and techniques to improve your proposal close ratio from an author who has mastered the fundamentals of writing winning sales proposals.

Greg Petras
Chairman & CEO, Involve Technology

Why read this book? Because it delivers results! Bob Kantin provides the tools and techniques to close more sales. And he convincingly makes the case why your sales force needs to invest their time to write winning proposals. The benefits are there for company and client alike.

David Talbot
Associate Publisher, *Wine Enthusiast Magazine*

Sales Professional's
Guide to
Writing Winning Proposals

A *What To Do About It Book*
from the
Why Johnny Can't Sell Series

Bob Kantin

BASCOM HILL PUBLISHING GROUP

For more information, contact Mill City Press, Inc., 212 3rd Avenue North, Suite 570, Minneapolis, MN 55401 or info@millcitypress.net

www.millcitypress.net

Cover designed by Jenni Wheeler

ISBN 0-9798467-2-2

ISBN 978-0-9798467-2-4

Printed in the United States of America

Dedication

This book is dedicated to Marylee, my wife, soul mate, and best friend. Thank you for your unwavering love, support, and encouragement.

Acknowledgement

Many thanks to Michael Nick, president and founder of ROI4Sales, Inc. and author of *ROI Selling*. Michael and I coauthored *Why Johnny Can't Sell ...and What to Do About It*. He suggested this book emphasize something that was obvious to us but perhaps not to others—developing and presenting sales proposals represents a process not a writing project. Based upon his suggestion and some of the innovative concepts we introduced in *Why Johnny Can't Sell*, this book explains why a winning, buyer-focused proposal represents a deliverable of two integrated processes, consultative selling and proposal development.

Contents

Foreword

When Bob Kantin and I started out writing the book *Why Johnny can't Sell ...and What to Do About It,* we wanted to create something very special that every sales rep, manager, and small business owner would use as a guide to better selling. Johnny's story was based loosely on a close friend of mine. He was once a great salesman; he had enormous success selling software solutions for IBM to Fortune 100 companies. Johnny could walk into a room full of strangers and walk out with a room full of new friends. The problem, however, is Johnny wouldn't have been able to *sell* a single thing to a single person. Why do you think this is true? Johnny's relationship-building skills were off of the charts, but his ability to analyze a situation, prescribe a solution, or help buyers make informed decisions were awful.

Johnny came to this realization when he met his new boss, Glen. Glen believed as Johnny, "relationships are the only way to sell." After all, "people buy from people," and that is all you need to know. Johnny was told: "you don't need sales training, a methodology, or sales tools to be successful. Just take them to lunch or go play golf and build a tight relationship." Johnny's handicap dropped almost as fast as his sales success. He called us after this revelation, and asked for our help.

The very first thing we did is try to understand Johnny's current situation. We gathered the facts around their sales process (or lack of one), sales methodology, sales tools, and sales training. We felt these four components, if working together will establish a backbone or framework for a success formula. Next, we created forms to identify gaps in their processes, tools, and training. (These same forms are available in *Why Johnny Can't Sell.*) Finally, we presented our findings and suggestions to Johnny and his management team. Johnny had a lot of internal selling to change the current management's mindset.

Our presentation consisted of a PowerPoint (presentation) of the process we used to identify their issues, pains and goals, findings and recommendations, and a proposal that included a detailed description of Johnny's current situation as we understood it, his current cost of this situation, and a comprehensive investment breakdown. For us to get to this point in the sales process, we felt it was necessary to use our sales methodology and sales tools to help us prove our theories and our value to Johnny and his management team. Each tool we used to assess Johnny's current situation moved us closer to our ultimate goal of a formal proposal presentation and, of course, a closed opportunity for us.

In this groundbreaking book, *Sales Professional's Guide to Writing Winning Proposals*, Bob details a framework to create a sales proposal that will shift the paradigm from typical sales person to sales professional. The days of filling out a simple one-page pricing sheet are long gone—they are being replaced by a sales proposal development process. This new process should become part of your success formula that includes analyzing your prospect's current situation, prescribing a solution, and assisting the buyer in making an informed decision. The concept of a sales proposal development process is supported by the fact that a buyer-focused sales proposal is the single biggest user of information gathered throughout the sales process.

This book is a practical roadmap that will help you understand how to leverage a winning sales proposal into more sales professionals achieving quota. Johnny's problems did not start and end with his proposal. Johnny's problems were leading up to the proposal and his lack of understanding for his customers' business issues, buying patterns, product impacts, and solution alternatives. Of course, his biggest problems were that he lacked of a winning sales proposal development process and a buyer-focused proposal model. Finally, by accepting the fact that sales proposal development is a process that needs as much or more attention than your sales process, you are on your way to a very successful and profitable career in sales. Remember, always sell your value, not your benefit.

Michael J. Nick
President of ROI4Sales, Inc.
Author: *ROI Selling*
Coauthor: *Why Johnny Can't Sell*
...and What to Do About It

Introduction

In *Why Johnny Can't Sell ...And What to Do About It,* Michael Nick and I presented our observations regarding why some sales professionals have problems selling in today's environment. Our primary goal was to help these sales professionals become better. We also wanted to help sales managers build better teams and CEOs get a better understanding of the sales process. Finally, we wanted to give sales professionals a few new ideas for doing things differently.

Our book took an uncommon view of sales. We devoted parts of the book to dissecting a generic consultative sales process. We discussed sales process phases and activities, the timing of activities, buyer information gathering, sales tool availability and use, and buyer interactions. We significantly expanded on a concept briefly mentioned in a book that I wrote several years ago—*Process Connections Information* (PCI). Our *Why Johnny Can't Sell* book included a matrix that graphically illustrated the interrelationships of time within sale process phases, the use of sales tools, PCI categories, and how sales tools are either sources or uses of PCI.

As we developed the matrix, it revealed something that I instinctively knew but never officially presented—sales proposals are the single biggest user of PCI. In other words, a well-written sales proposal contains most of the important buyer-specific information gathered and acted upon during a consultative sales process. Our matrix clearly defined which sales tools were needed as sources of buyer information that would eventually be used in a custom sales proposal. The matrix also clearly revealed the need to integrate two processes—consultative sales and proposal development.

I decided to write another book on how to write winning sales proposals. However, this new book uses the matrix from the *Why Johnny Can't Sell* book to show the links between sales tools and each main section of a sales proposal. And, it presents my proven, five-section proposal structure in the context of the matrix. In other words, for the first time sales professionals can understand what to include in a winning sales proposal, why to include it, and which sales tools are needed to gather the PCI contained in each proposal section.

This new book presents the concept that developing a winning sales proposal is a process not a single-event, writing project. It shows that sales organizations and sales professionals will continue to experience mediocre results if they view proposal development as simply a cutting and pasting exercise using past proposals. And, as discussed in *Why Johnny Can't Sell ...and What to Do About It,* this book also affirms the need for a sales organization to take responsibility for developing and maintaining proposal models for its sales force.

How to Use this Book

Read the first three chapters of this book to learn why many companies and their sales professionals struggle to write sales proposals. Discover if your company reflects some of the myths and realities discussed in the first chapter. Read Chapter 2 to understand how and why consultative selling and proposal development must be integrated processes. Learn about the purposes of a sales proposal in Chapter 3 and if you haven't read *Why Johnny Can't Sell ...and What to Do About It,* this chapter introduces a condensed version of the matrix.

Read Chapters 4 through 12 to get a concise blueprint for designing and developing winning, buyer-focused sales proposals. Chapter 4 provides an overview of what to include and why to include it. The next five chapters cover my five recommended main proposal sections. These five chapters also include the matrix with the highlighted PCI categories and sales tools for each proposal section. Chapter 10 explains how and why to write an executive summary and transmittal letter. Read Chapter 11 to learn how to develop a compelling title page, use your word processing system to generate a table of contents, and effectively use appendices to control the length of the proposal. Finally, read Chapter 12 to get packaging ideas for your new proposal.

If you want to write shorter or smaller proposals, read Chapter 13. It will give you instructions for writing sales proposals in letter format. However, you'll have to read Chapters 4 through 9 first because a letter proposal also uses the flow of information and ideas provided by my five section structure.

The last chapter discusses the need to create a sales proposal development process. It includes a blank matrix to help you identify the sales tools needed by your organization, which represent the sources of PCI for your sales proposals. This chapter also includes directions for developing sales proposal models using one of your actual customer proposals as the starting point. You'll want to read Chapter 14 to determine if automating proposal production makes sense for your company.

Who Should Read this Book?

I think there are audiences for this book beyond the sales professional who has to write his or her own proposals because the company doesn't provide approved sales proposal models. The others who would benefit from this book include:

- *Vice President of Sales.* Learn how and why providing your sales force with winning, buyer-focused sales proposal models can reap tremendous rewards. Understand how and why to integrate your sales and proposal development processes. Determine if your company would benefit by automating the proposal production process.

- *Vice President of Marketing.* Learn how you can help the sales department design top-notch customer communications documents called sales proposals. Also, understand why you should help sales generate proposals that align with your branding initiative.

- *Product Management/Support.* Understand how you can help the sales department better and more accurately present your product (or service) and its features and benefits.

- *Professional Services.* Learn how you can help the sales department and ultimately your own staff and operations by accurately defining your implementation methodology in the company's sales proposals.

- *CEOs.* Understand what should be happening in your sales department—why your company should be providing its sales force with company-approved proposal models. Learn how increasing your company's *proposal close ratio* can dramatically increase revenues with minimal increases to incremental costs.

Who Is Johnny?

The Johnny who appears at the beginning of most chapters in this book is the same person from the book *Why Johnny Can't Sell ...and What to Do About It.* Eight months have passed since Johnny accepted the position of Sales Director for a new division of a twenty-year-old company. He has been successful at growing the division and his hired several sales professionals.

Because of competitive pressures and a recent loss, Johnny and his team have realized that their sales proposals aren't working. The proposal model Johnny originally developed for the new division was nothing more than pieces of proposals from other divisions that he cut and pasted together. He and his sales team are starting to realize that their proposal is not much more than a price quote surrounded by a poorly written brochure. Johnny has initiated a project to design and develop a winning proposal model or models.

1

Stop Lying to Yourself: Myths and Realities

Eight months after he started, Johnny is still excited about his new company. The new product he was hired to sell is doing well. He's added five new sales professionals to his sales team and will add two more in the next several months. He's made sure that his sales team is made up of experienced professionals. Like Johnny, they've gone through the company's standard week in product training. They've learned about the functions, features, and benefits of the company's products and how the professional services team does business.

Johnny realized shortly after he joined the company that management thinks everyone sells consultatively, but in reality there's no "company-approved" sales process. Everyone, including his team, tends to do their own thing. Some of his team members meticulously document findings and agreements reached with their prospective customers in letters or emails. Others aren't quite as disciplined. The good news is that overall the team is doing well.

Over the past few months, Johnny and his team have been working on a project. They're trying to reach consensus on one question, "Why would a company buy our products and services?" The purpose of the project is to change the focus of sales activities from primarily dealing with technical requirements to better understanding a buyer's business issues and the impact the company's products and services could have on them. Johnny soon realized that the project will significantly change how his team sells. If successful, the project will help his team identify the issues, pains, or goal their prospects might be facing. More important, it should help them define what it takes to motivate and persuade a buyer's decision makers. When Johnny started at the company, his boss Dave and Sara, the director of corporate marketing, gave him some sample sales proposals developed by sales professionals from the other divisions. He thought some of them were pretty good. So he "cut and pasted" pieces from several proposals to build one for his new product. The first time each team members needed to write a proposal, he gave them the "model" and told him to make it fit the situation.

Now, after several weeks on the project to understand "why companies buy their products and services," Johnny is beginning to think that their sales proposals are woefully inadequate. He understands that their proposals are totally disconnected from the sales process and do little to help buyers make informed buying decisions. The bad news for Johnny is that he just has identified a new problem for his team. The good news—at least he recognizes it.

Many companies selling complex products or services have to write sales proposals to close business. Their proposals can range from a simple price quote to a few pages in letter format to a formal proposal of ten to fifteen pages or more. Seems like it should be a simple process to communicate in writing what had been discussed in meetings, presentations, and demonstrations. But, most sales professionals hate writing proposals. Ever wonder why?

Observations of the Current Situation

Here are some observations I have made about how companies and sales professionals perceive sales proposals:

- If you ask sales professionals to describe their proposal writing process in one word, they respond as follows: *daunting, tedious, frustrating, distracting,* and *unproductive.*

- Most sales professionals write their own proposals; very rarely does a company provide its sales force with "company-approved" proposal models or templates. *Cutting and pasting* is considered a writing style.

- Closely related to the previous observation, no one in the sales organization has responsibility for proposal content let alone format, structure, and packaging.

- Sales professionals often take an inordinate amount of time to produce mediocre sales proposals. It's not uncommon for sales professionals to spend four to six hours or more writing proposals— a very expensive activity.

- Few companies measure their *Proposal Close Ratios*, which provide a good way to evaluate the effectiveness of sales proposals in the sales process—one has to measure the activity to manage it.

- Most companies and sales professionals simply view sales proposals as just another necessary document needed to close a deal. They treat it as a writing project rather than as a *proposal development process*, which should be integrated with their consultative sales process.

Myths

Here are some myths about writing and producing sales proposals— *the documents we give the buyer's decision makers.*

Myth #1: Sales professionals have good written communications skills

Most sales professionals have good oral communications skills. They stand up in front of groups and deliver presentations and do demonstrations—most really like performing and do it extremely well. But written communications skills are totally different. Unless they took business writing courses in college, most sales professionals don't write very good (or is it well?). Actually, many people, except for journalism and English majors, don't like to write more than a short email.

So, if you think your sales professionals are writing quality proposals, think again; they're probably not. More than likely they are writing or cutting and pasting long, boring pages of text that most decision makers won't read.

Myth #2: Every sales professional can generate professional-looking proposals

The term "professional-looking" is relative. Most people will say their sales proposals look professional; however, the reality is most aren't. To make any document professional-looking requires skills dealing with structure, format, and layout. Most sales professionals lack skills in these areas.

Another closely related factor in this area is how well sales proposal writers, the sales professionals, can use the myriad of features in their word-processing systems. For many, a word-processing system is not much more than an electronic typewriter with lots of memory. That's why I see so many poor quality documents—cutting and pasting from several documents can really create formatting challenges for the untrained user.

In reality, the buyer is the ultimate judge whether a sales proposal is professional-looking. Perhaps, today's buyers have high expectation because they're constantly exposed to high-quality Web sites, brochures, and other print media. When they get a poor quality sales proposal, it sends a subliminal, negative message about the selling organization—*If their proposals are this bad, is their service any better?*

```
For example, what would your first
impression be of a proposal if it were
printed in the font used in this
paragraph? Buyers expect quality from the
companies with which they do business.
And, a sales proposal often is the first
deliverable from the seller to the
prospective buyer's decision makers.
```

If your sales professionals are writing their own proposals, take a look at some of them. Be honest, do they look like professional documents or something someone threw together? One VP of Sales once told me he thought some of his sales professionals should use crayons to write their proposals.

Myth #3: Our company has some great boilerplate proposal models

Boilerplate proposal models make proposal writing easy for sales professionals. To write a proposal, one simply inserts the prospect's name using the "find and replace" feature in the word-processing system and then inserts the proposed price, and some project dates. It's done and ready for printing.

Some companies actually have centralized sales support functions that do this work. They plug in the variables and produce the proposals for the sales professionals—it just doesn't get any easier than this. The company controls the message, production, and packaging. Two big problems: 1) most decision makers can spot a boilerplate proposal when they see one and 2) boilerplate proposals are totally incompatible with any consultative sales process.

Myth #4: Our sales proposals are tightly integrated into our consultative sales process (perhaps the biggest myth of all)

Here's this myth's logic from many companies' viewpoints:

We send all of our new sales professionals to one of the consultative sales training seminars; therefore, their sales proposals must reflect the results of their consultative sales activities.

This appears to be sound logic, but in reality, it's usually false. Sending people to consultative sales training doesn't make them consultative sales professionals and it doesn't mean that they know how or why their sales proposals should be integrated into the sales process—some consultative sales methodologies simply have a timeline that indicates when to write a proposal. Ironically, sales professionals who do sell consultatively gain a wealth of information about their buyers. However, most don't know how or why to use this information effectively in their proposal development processes.

Realities

Reality #1: Producing a winning, buyer-focused sales proposal is a process, NOT a writing project

Selling consultatively is an essential ingredient for writing winning, buyer-focused sales proposals. As a sales professional works with the buyer, he must identify and define the buyer information contained in his sales proposal. Think about all the activities that take place in a well-executed consultative sales process. A sales professional often works with one or two people from the buyer's organization—key contacts. Key contacts influence the buying decision, but they usually don't make it. Therefore, everything discussed and agreed to with the contacts needs to be communicated to the decision makers for their review. A well-written sales proposal should contain everything, all the information gathered and processed during the sales process, that a decision maker needs to make an informed business decision.

Some of the key components of the proposal are completed at various times during a consultative sales process. For example, a sales professional shouldn't be gathering and defining critical buyer information when he's writing the proposal. Rather, during the sales process, a sales professional should:

- Identify the buyer's critical business issues and their impact on its business

* Match buyer needs to product benefits and service capabilities
* Define the financial justification
* Develop preliminary plans for implementing the proposed product or service
* Learn what will mitigate the buyer's risk for buying and making a change

A sales professional will recognize that these sales activities also are needed to develop sales proposals (more about this in Chapters 2 and 3). If he's designed a buyer-focused sales proposal model, the buyer information requirements of the model also help define the activities of his proposal development process. Therefore, to write buyer-focused sales proposals, a sales professional must integrate sales and proposal development. He can't treat the proposal as just a writing project.

Reality #2: It's the buyer's decision-making document

A selling organization calls it a sales proposal, because it may represent a deliverable that signals the end of a sales process phase. However, to the buyer a sales proposal probably starts a phase in its buying process. The proposal becomes the document that its decision makers use to make a buying decision. More important for the seller, a well-written proposal connects the selling organization and the results of its sales process with the buyer's decision makers during their buying process.

The buyer expects that a seller's sales proposal will provide them with all the information they need to make an informed decision. If it doesn't, a poorly written sales proposal can put the sale, or more precisely, the buying decision, at risk. The risk doesn't reflect the quality of the seller's proposed product or service. Rather, the sale is put at risk because the seller's proposal doesn't contain all of the information, or the right information, that the buyer's decision makers need. They probably don't feel convinced enough to make the decision, which often means delayed sale or NO SALE.

And What to Do About It

Myths #1 and #2 indicate that most sales professionals probably don't have all of the skills needed to write winning proposals. Myth #3 debunks the use of boilerplate proposals as a viable solution and Myth #4 indicates training sales professionals to sell consultatively is no guarantee that their proposals will reflect the results of the process. So what works? Here are some things I have found that will help a company and its sales professionals produce winning, buyer-focused sales proposals, or buyer decision-making documents:

- Make sure the sales proposal development process integrates and reinforces a consultative sales process
- Develop custom, buyer-focused sales proposal models proposals
- Automate sales proposal production

Make sure the sales proposal development process integrates and reinforces a consultative sales process

I have found that if sales professionals have been trained to sell consultatively, then it's easy for them to gather and define the buyer information required by their proposal models. Equally important, the sales proposal models provided by their companies provide places to use the buyer information gathered and defined.

This integration and reinforcement may sound easy but it takes some planning and design. A winning, buyer-focused sales proposal will require sales professionals to follow and integrate their consultative selling and proposal development processes. Their sales proposals must use the terms and labels used in the sales process. For example, if a consultative sales process trains sales professionals to define "critical business issues," then the proposal models each should have a subsection with that title.

Therefore, a company must:

- Customize and integrate its sales and proposal development processes for the products or services it sells and how it sells.
- Develop custom proposal models that integrate and reinforce the processes.

Develop custom sales proposal models

It's very effective to design sales proposal models in which the buyer information requirements reinforce (or force) consultative selling activities. In other words, the buyer information requirements of the proposal models require sales professionals to ask some pertinent questions and reach preliminary agreements with the buyer. This also prepares sales professionals to make some educated decisions about the application and resulting value proposition of the proposed product or service—activities of the proposal development process.

Custom sales proposal models also should reflect the company's decisions regarding structure, content, and format. This will reinforce the company's branding initiative, which will make the VP of marketing very happy.

Automate proposal production

Automating proposal production saves time and money because sales professionals typically can generate top-notch proposals in minutes not hours (or days) using an automated system. Equally important, automated proposal production systems ensure quality and consistency of output. Most systems generate sales proposals in word-processing document format so sales professionals don't have to do much more than print the document after it's generated—no cutting and pasting and the associated formatting problems.

Here's the Bottom Line

If you expect Johnny or your sales professionals to produce winning, buyer-focused sales proposals that read like they were written by an English major and look like they were designed by a graphic artist, you'll be disappointed 99.5 percent of the time. Get your sales professionals out of the mindset that writing a proposal is a project. Get them to: 1) view proposal development as a process with defined buyer information requirements and 2) understand that the proposal development process includes defined process activities. Finally, make sure they have the custom sales tools and systems needed to do their jobs.

Stuff to Remember

In this chapter, I identified many of the sales proposal myths and realities that Johnny's company and many other companies experience. Johnny's project of trying to reach consensus on one question, "Why would a company buy our products and services?" is going to be most beneficial as he and his team develop winning sales proposals.

√ Producing a sales proposal is a process, NOT a writing project.

√ Many companies expect their sales professionals to write their own proposal—no one in a company is responsible for developing "company-approved" proposal models.

√ A sales proposal typically signals the end of a process phase for the seller. However, to the buyer, it represents a decision-making document in its buying process.

√ Boilerplate proposal models make proposal writing easy for sales professionals. One big problem, most decision makers can spot a boilerplate proposal when they see one.

√ To produce winning, buyer-focused sales proposals —buyer decision-making documents— consider: 1) Developing custom sales proposal models proposals, 2) Making sure your sales proposal models integrate and reinforce your consultative sales process, and 3) Automating sales proposal production.

2

Integrating the Processes: Selling and Proposal Development

Scott, one of Johnny's sales professionals, just said he lost a big deal that he had been working on for several months. He thought he had done everything right: qualifying, validating the product with demonstrations, confirming available budget, writing the proposal, and presenting it to the buying committee. He even did another product demo after the presentation. He had been confident everyone really liked the product.

Besides losing a big commission check, Scott was taking it personally. After all, he had developed good rapport and relationship with his contact. They had shared several lunches and even attended a baseball game with their wives. All the buying signs had been there.

But, the competitor got the deal and it hurt. Scott said his contact was reluctant to tell him why he didn't get the deal. However, he did say the committee felt that the competitor seemed to understand their business issues and situation better, particularly the business side of the equation. The committee realized the two competing products would work, yet they just felt more confident selecting the competitor. As a parting comment, Scott's contact did mention that the competitor had done a better job on its proposal and presentation—significantly better.

A winning proposal is all about the buyer. It should focus on the buyer's business, its critical business issues, and its needs. To write a buyer-focused proposal, you need to work closely with the buyer during your sales process. This means you should act more like a consultant and less like a salesperson. If you start treating the buyer like a client to whom you're consulting, the buyer may start treating you like a business consultant.

Selling Like a Consultant

Consultative selling dictates how a sales professional consults with a buyer to determine such things as:

- The buyer's current situation and the business issues they are facing that affect the business

- What the buyer needs to do, to change, or to acquire to improve the business and resolve the business issues

- How the proposed product can work for the buyer

- How the buyer can benefit from buying the product, including how much it can reduce or avoid costs or increase revenues

You need to use a custom consultative sales process to write the kinds of proposals I describe in this book. Actually, you're going to realize that the customer information requirements of your proposals can help you sell more consultatively. In other words, you'll sell consultatively when you gather and define the buyer information needed to write the kind of sales proposals described in this book.

Consultative Selling + Proposal Development

To write better proposals and get more business, you need to integrate two processes: consultative selling and proposal development. Some sales people think a sales proposal is simply a document that is written at some point in a sales process—just another writing project. I think proposal development is a process itself complete with activities and milestones. *Proposal development* is the process you use to design, write, and produce sales proposals.

When you follow a consultative sales process, you end up knowing a lot about your customers. And, with better and broader customer information, you write better proposals. As you write better proposals, you logically become a better gatherer of information from your potential customers. It's integrated and circular—the consultative sales process leads to better proposals and better proposals reinforce your consultative sales process.

Consultative selling requires analyzing that part of the buyer's business that relates to your proposed product. (In this book, I'll just use *product* when I mean either a product or a service.) It also means giving the buyer all the information that it needs to make an informed buying decision *before* you give it the actual sales proposal. Your sales proposal may document the results of your consultative selling activities. But, it's more than just the document; it's about your integrated processes.

Johnny's project in which he and his team are trying to reach consensus on one question, "Why would a company buy our products and services?" makes perfect sense. He wants to change the focus of sales activities from primarily dealing with technical requirements to better understanding a buyer's business issues and the impact from their company's products and services. This certainly represents one aspect of consultative selling and provides the foundation for a buyer-focused sales proposal.

Proposal Content Can Define Sales Consulting Activities

You can work backwards from your proposal to determine what types of consultative sales activities are needed. When you develop proposal models, you know up front what your proposal will contain. For example, if your proposal model contains sophisticated value justification information, then you know that your sales process needs to include gathering customer data to calculate the value justification. In this case, the proposal's content actually defines some very specific consultative selling activities—by working backwards from the proposal, you know that you need to gather and analyze your buyer's current costs.

Integrating your consultative sales and proposal development processes can result in this type of reverse engineering. In other words, identifying what you're going to put in your sales proposal defines some of your selling activities. Your proposal's content actually helps you decide what information you need to get from a buyer and what you need to do with it; you design—or reverse engineer—some of your consultative sales process activities using your proposal as the basis for your design.

When you integrate your consultative sales and proposal development processes, you find some buyer information that connects or is common to the two processes. I call this *process connections information* (PCI). PCI represents those areas where consultative selling and proposal development activities overlap. These connections are in two main areas:

- **Buyer information:** Information you need to know about the buyer to understand its business, issues, and needs.

- **Application of your product:** How your proposed product will work in the buyer's business and the resulting benefits including how much: 1) money it will save, 2) expenses it will avoid, or 3) revenues it will generate.

In Figure 2-1, you can see how this idea of process connections information works. The information requirements of your consultative sales process overlap with the information requirements of your proposal development process. The overlap area defines two things:

- **Common buyer information** the *process connections information* gathered and used in both processes

- **Common sales and proposal development activities** that must be completed to develop winning, buyer-focused sales proposals and to sell consultatively—*common activities*

Several years ago I was doing a rollout of a new proposal model for one of our clients. This client kept a sales trainer under contract to train new hires and periodically deliver refresher training to the entire sales force. He was invited to attend our rollout session. After the session he said, "I have been training the sales professionals to collect much of the buyer information you included in the new proposal model—now I have a place to put it."

Figure 2-1 Integrated Process with Common Activities and Information

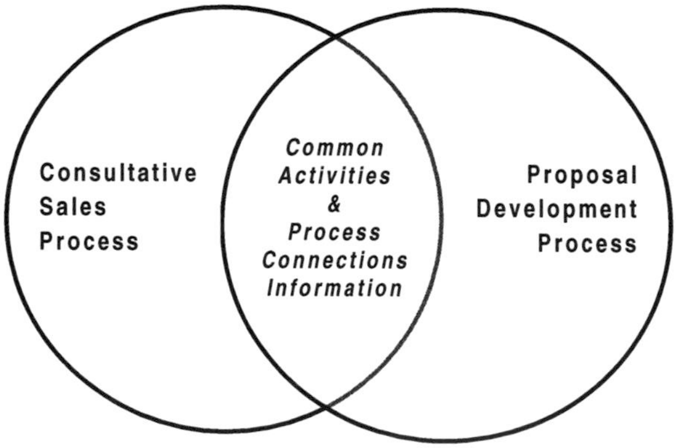

More about Process Connections Information

In our book, *Why Johnny Can't Sell ...and What to Do About It,* Michael Nick and I introduced the concept of *process connections information* (PCI). Here's an excerpt from our book that defines PCI.

The more time a sales professional spends with a prospective buyer, and the more questions asked and answered, the more knowledge he gains—unless he's not asking the right questions or capturing the information. Sometimes certain categories of prospect information are needed to initiate the next sales phase. For instance, a sales professional can't complete the presentation phase or perform an ROI value estimation without identifying, capturing, and confirming the prospect's key issues, challenges, and goals.

Common prospective customer information often links sales phases and sales tools. We call this common customer information Process Connections Information (PCI). There are several reasons it is important to understand PCI and its linkages:

- The PCI linkages between sales phases enable and ensure a logical progression of prospect information-gathering throughout the sales process.
- Defining the PCI linkages between sales processes and sales tools assures the required information is gathered at the appropriate times and available for use when needed, either by another sales tool or in subsequent sales process phases.
- When identifying gaps in a custom sales tool kit, one needs to understand the PCI that links individual sales tools to each other and the availability requirements of specific PCI throughout the entire sales process.

Customer relationship management (CRM) and sales force automation (SFA) systems should contain some of the process connections information gathered and used during the sales process. In Tom Siebel's book, *Virtual Selling,* he states, "In the future, the value of a corporation will be best measured by its knowledge of its customers, its knowledge of markets, and its knowledge of its own products. Therein will lay the company's competitive power." By including process connections information in your CRM or SFA system, you can:

- facilitate or reinforce the consultative sales process,

> - provide a prospect information database for the entire organization to access,
> - develop high-quality best practices for customer correspondence and other sales process documents,
> - compliment your market analysis and provide detailed feedback to marketing,
> - capture market information used to assess sales strategy and goals, and complete a more accurate sales forecast.

Some of the process connections information that you use in your proposal development process might include:

- General buyer information

- Critical business issues regarding the buyer's current situation and their impact on the business

- Product or service application: how the proposed product or service works in the buyer's business

- Buyer benefits: the financial and non-financial benefits that the buyer receives from the product or service

- Implementation: how and when the product will be implemented and what the buyer's involvement is

The Pitch for Connecting Two Essential Processes

When you put the consultative sales and proposal development processes together correctly, they produce outstanding results. Combining them makes you a more effective sales professional because your customers think that you really know what you're talking about. They start looking to you for some answers to tough questions. If you treat your sales proposals as a key deliverable of the integrated processes, your proposals do a much better job selling and representing your company and its products.

Let me explain the concept a little bit more by describing what happens when the processes are *not* integrated:

- **Consultative selling not integrated with proposal development.** In most sales situations, if you consistently follow consultative selling practices but neglect to integrate your sales and your proposal development processes, you can still win a reasonable amount of business. But you're probably missing some sales. Your proposals are probably pretty average; maybe you just write boilerplate proposals. Buyers may think that your proposals are disconnected from your sales process. They most likely think that you're a good business consultant during the sales process, but that you drop the ball when it comes to following through in your sales proposals.

- **Proposal development not integrated into consultative selling.** If you spend a lot of energy on writing sales proposals and are really good at it, but don't follow good consultative selling practices, you also miss closing some business. You probably don't spend enough time learning about a buyer's business and understanding its business issues. You may be skipping some critical process steps. You may jump the gun and write a proposal way too early—the buyer isn't ready to receive a proposal and you aren't ready to write one.

Sales Proposal as a Process Crutch

Some sales professionals use the sales proposal as a crutch. They move too quickly to write a proposal because they think the buyer is ready or because they have very good proposal models to use. Their proposals include some good reasons for a buyer to make a change, but they're generic reasons—they don't really fit the buyer's exact situation. They lack the depth that comes from really understanding the buyer's business and knowing exactly how your product can reduce or avoid costs or increase revenues. The proposals just don't seem to exactly apply to the situation. These sales professionals need to step back, slow down, and become more consultative.

Stuff to Remember

Johnny was starting to think he and his team were on the right track and perhaps going in the right direction. He was starting to see how changing the focus of their sales process was going to change how they developed sales proposals.

√ If you want to write better proposals and get more business, integrate two processes: consultative selling and proposal development.

√ You can work backwards from your proposal models to determine what types of consultative sales activities are needed. When you develop proposal models, you know up front what your proposal will contain.

√ When you integrate consultative sales and proposal development processes, you find some buyer information connects the two processes—*process connections information* (PCI)—and the collection of PCI typically represent activities that overlap—*common activities.*

If you treat your sales proposals as a key deliverable of the integrated processes (consultative selling and proposal development), your proposals do a much better job selling and representing your company and its products.

3

Purposes of a Proposal—the Process that Glues It Altogether

Johnny learned that Scott, one of his sales professionals, had recently lost a big deal. Scott said he had become good friends with his contact, so losing to a competitor also was difficult to accept personally. However, after analyzing the situation and reflecting on some comments that his contact had made, Scott told Johnny that he thought the major reason he lost the deal was because his sales proposal was second-rate. From a price standpoint, his proposal was about 3 percent less than the competitor's price—so price wasn't the issue.

Johnny wasn't too surprised when Scott said his proposal was a key issue in the buyer's decision. Over the past few months, Johnny and his team have been working on a project trying to reach consensus on one question, "Why would a company buy our products and services?" The project now started to take on a clearer focus. After reading Scott's proposal, it was obvious that it didn't address the buyer's business issues and needs. More important, it didn't discuss the impact of the proposed product on the buyer's business. He could see how a more buyer-focused proposal could educate and motivate buyer's decision makers—perhaps the competitor's proposal had.

Johnny started to understand the linkages between consultative selling and developing a winning proposal. Unfortunately, Scott had started with a proposal model Johnny gave all the sales professionals. Now Johnny and his team needed to develop a new and better model. And he knew it needed to be more than someplace to stick the price, product specs, and information about the company.

Think about all the sales activities that a sales professional completes in the sales process leading up to the point where the buyer is ready to make a decision. Perhaps the sales professional has given the buyer some or all of the following documents:

- Business development letter
- Brochures
- Data sheets
- Confirmation letters
- ROI valuation
- Systems configuration
- Demonstration results
- Case studies
- Preliminary price or fee quote
- Customer and reference lists
- Implementation plan

When the buyer is ready to make a decision, its decision makers probably won't sort through all this stuff. They'll expect a written proposal from the seller—something that pulls it all together. More important, they'll expect a proposal to provide them with a logical flow of information and ideas on which to make an informed buying decision.

Sales Proposals Defined

A *sales proposal* is the seller's written plan or offer presented to a buyer to exchange property, goods, or services for money. The buyer either accepts or rejects the proposal. Naturally, you hope the buyer accepts!

Many companies (and people) use sales proposals in their normal course of business. Some companies write sales proposals to sell very costly and complex products or services. For example, a computer system consulting firm that develops e-commerce applications has to write proposals to get signed contracts. Its sales and proposal development processes may have lasted several months and required many sales calls by the sales professional and others from the consulting firm. These processes probably included very detailed analyses of some parts of the customer's business.

For costly or complex sales, the seller's proposed product often is an important, high-dollar purchase for the buyer. Because of the cost and complexity of the purchase, one person probably often can't make the buying decision. Rather, an executive or buying committee makes the final buying decision. They need a written proposal on which to base their buying decision.

Most proposals are proactive

At some point during the sales process the buyer may ask for a proposal. Although the buyer initiates the request, the seller has been actively working with the buyer to get to the point where the buyer wants and needs a proposal to make a decision. This represents a *proactive* proposal because the seller has been actively working with the buyer to get it to a point in the sales process where it asks for a proposal.

However, there also are *reactive* proposals out there. A reactive proposal is one where the buyer, usually an organization, formally asks the seller (or a group of sellers) for a proposal by issuing a request for proposal or RFP. The selling organization or the sales professional may not have had any previous contact with the buyer, but he reacts to its proposal request by writing a proposal—an RFP response.

The VP of sales for one of our clients that delivers custom training programs called to get our thoughts on RFPs. He said that they periodically will get an RFP from a company that they were not actively pursuing. Typically, these RFPs were for substantial engagements so they were always interested in responding. I asked how often he won one of the deals. He said, "Not very often, if ever."

I stated that his company is one of the high-price providers for training services in its specific field. This means that unless his company can really differentiate itself and its training programs from the competition in its RFP response, the deal will probably go to one of the lower-priced competitors.

Further, I told him that he should look at the RFP from the viewpoint of a sales person working for one of the competitors. His prospect has to get competitive bids, so the competitor's sales person tells his prospect to send an RFP to your company. He knows that your price would be much higher; so his chances of winning are vastly improved.

The VP of Sales said, "You're right, we're probably just column-fodder!" My response was, "Yeah, you probably are, but continue to closely evaluate each RFP. Most important, if the unsolicited RFP doesn't allow you to meet with the prospect, decline the opportunity to respond."

Satisfying the Buyer's Need for Information

Your proposal serves two important purposes, whether it's just a short proposal in letter format or a thirty-page, written offer to sell an expensive, complex product. The proposal is a:

- **Customer communications document.** Your written plan or offer to the buyer to exchange your product or service for money

- **Buyer decision-making document.** A document for the buyer's review and analysis from which to make an informed buying decision

Customer communications document

If you get most of your business through your proposals, they may be one of your most important forms of customer communications—more important than your brochures, magazine and newspaper ads, press releases, and your Web site. Although brochures and other customer communications can attract sales leads, they can't close sales. It usually takes a sales professional and a buyer-focused sales proposal to help the buyer make an informed buying decision.

Buyer decision-making document

It's tough for some people to make a decision, especially one that involves a lot of money or is really important for their company. They need to have something to read and study. They want to scribble notes on it or write some questions in its margins.

Here's something to think about: If a proposal is a buyer's decision-making tool, then the better it's written, the better the buyer will feel about making the decision to buy the product. When developing a proposal, always put yourself in the decision maker's place. What would you want and need to know? What would it take to make you feel good about your buying decision? Here are some questions you might ask if you were in that position:

- How can it reduce costs or avoid costs or increase revenues?

- Does this product meet our company's needs?

- How will the product work in our unique business operation? In other words, what's its application?

- How will our company benefit, financially and non-financially, from implementing the product?

- What process does the seller use, and how long will it take, to implement the product for our company?

- What makes the organization selling the product a good choice for our company?

Selling to Top Management

In most sales situations, the senior managers from the buyer's organization read your sales proposals—usually the people who make the final buying decisions. In many cases, you may have limited or no contact with these decision makers. Your primary contact with the buyer, usually a department or project manager, may keep you from talking directly with top management. Many times, you don't get to present your proposal. Instead, your contact sends all the competitive proposals to the decision makers for their review and schedules a meeting to make a decision. Even if you've developed good rapport and built a solid relationship with your contact, that doesn't make any difference to the people making the decision. Your proposal is all that they're looking at. The proposal represents your deal and your company.

To an informed decision maker, the winning proposal isn't always the one with the lowest price. The winning proposal may be the one that did the best job of educating the buyer. Or, it may be the one that presented the most compelling, buyer-specific reasons to make a change. Or maybe the winning proposal is the one that did a great job differentiating the winning company from the competition.

The Proposal—the Biggest Process Connections Information User

In the first two chapters, I stated that selling consultatively is an essential ingredient for writing winning, buyer-focused sales proposals. As a sales professional works with the buyer, he will identify and define the *process connections information* (PCI), which belongs in a sales proposal. It's important to note that:

- A sales proposal is the sales tool that is the single biggest user of PCI.

- Many of the activities used to gather the PCI needed in a proposal development process are common with the activities and processes in a consultative sales process—*common activities*.

Figure 3-1 is an extract of a large matrix from my book, *Why Johnny Can't Sell ...and What to Do About It.* The full matrix shows the interrelationships and timing of sales process phases, sales tools, and process connections information. This matrix only shows some of the sales tools that are sources (S) of PCI, used (U) in the sales proposal.

Take some time to study the matrix. Think about the activities a sales professional must complete to gather or define the PCI needed in a sales proposal. Note that some of these tools and activities are common to consultative selling and developing sales proposals.

For example, a sales professional might use a "Buyer Questionnaire" to help her collect the specific PCI requirements needed to sell consultatively and develop a buyer-focused sales proposal. The PCI contained in the questionnaire represents required content for the sales proposal and also required information needed to sell consultatively. Perhaps it's even more critical for developing the proposal because some of the PCI will end up in a document sent to the buyer.

Figure 3-1 Sources of PCI Used in a Sales Proposal

Sales Tools	Process Connections Information									
	Background Information	Critical Business Issues, KPIs	Impacts on Business	Customer Stated Needs	Customer's Selection Criteria	Product/Service Application	Prices/Fees	Non-Financial Benefits	Financial Benefits	Implementation/ Installation Variables
Customer Intelligence	S	S								
Customer's Web Site	S	S								
Prospect Survey	S	S		S	S					
Buyer Questionnaire	S	S	S	S	S					
KPI Input (Key Pain Indicator)	U	S		S						
Pricing/Configure System		U		U		S	S			S
ROI Valuation	U	S	S	S		U	U		S	
Sales Process Letters (various)	U	U	U	U	U	U	U	S	U	U
Sales Proposal	U	U	U	U	U	U	U	U	U	U

Some Key Purposes of a Sales Proposal

Besides *gluing it altogether* for the buyer, a sales proposal has several additional key purposes:

* Matches needs to benefits
* Defines financial justification
* Reduces risk

Matches needs to benefits

Selling consultatively includes defining a buyer's needs. Some consultative sales methodologies consider a buyer's needs to represent its ideas for a solution. Therefore, if you can clearly define a buyer's needs, what the buyer thinks represents a solution, you can match those needs to the benefits provided by your product features or service capabilities. In other words, by clearly defining the buyer's needs in your proposal, you can "set the stage" for your proposed product and its value proposition. If done correctly, you can position your product as a perfect fit for the prospective customer.

The effective use of PCI in the proposal development process results in a compelling deliverable—a winning, buyer-focused proposal. If defining buyer needs represents a required activity of the proposal development process, then matching buyer's needs to product benefits represents a supporting and, therefore, required activity. You'll learn in Chapter 6, Proposing Your Solution, how to convert generic product benefits into buyer-specific benefits—another important activity in the proposal development process.

Defines financial justification

One of the most important purposes of a proposal is to describe how your proposed product reduces expenses, avoids costs, or increases revenues—more PCI stuff. A sales proposal should specifically identify and explain the money-saving or money-making benefits the buyer will realize. Your custom return on investment (ROI) valuation uses the prospect's key pain indicators (KPIs) as a basis for these calculations. This buyer-specific ROI information belongs in a sales proposal. Obviously, you can't convince a decision maker of your product's financial benefits using industry averages, vague examples, or constructed case studies.

One would expect that developing a financial justification represents a required activity of a consultative selling process. Interestingly, this is not the case for some companies. However, as you will read in Chapter 6, Proposing Your Solution, a sales proposal that lacks solid financial justification may not provide convincing reasons for a decision maker to make a buy decision. Therefore, I consider developing a financial justification a required activity of a sales proposal development process.

Reduces buyer risk

Most buyers face risk when making a change. For example, implementing a new system, installing a new machine, or hiring a new (and unknown) consulting firm all represent decisions that carry risk. Business risk becomes a factor in the decision process because most companies aren't eager to jeopardize their success. Your contacts and the decision makers also have personal risk for recommending or making a wrong decision. Therefore, to reduce the buyer's business and personal risk, a proposal must present some information about the seller and its capabilities—it must assure the buyer that the seller is experienced and can deliver on the contract.

During the sales process, you try to identify buyer's concerns that may prevent it from making the proposed change. You should note specific buyer's concerns and, if possible, make sure that your proposal adequately addresses each. If you follow a consultative sales process, you should learn what concerns the buyer has about making a change.

Your sales proposal must assure a buyer of your company's capabilities. A proposal's general appearance and its overall quality will send subtle messages to the buyer. Its flow of information and ideas, writing style, format, paper quality, and binding tell the buyer a lot about the selling organization. Therefore, your proposal development process has to address content design issues and the physical production of the proposal itself.

Stuff to Remember

In this chapter, Johnny and his team learned that a winning sales proposal has to be more than a price quote surrounded by technical specifications and company hype. Everyone was starting to understand that their sales proposals should contain pertinent buyer information, include a solid value justification, and help mitigate the risk that a buyer might have for making a change.

√ Your proposal serves two important purposes: a customer communication document from the seller and the buyer's decision-making document.

√ A sales proposal represents the single biggest user of *process connections information* (PCI).

√ Many of the activities or sub-processes used to gather the PCI needed in a proposal are common with the activities and processes in a consultative sales process—*common activities*.

 Besides gluing it all together for the buyer, a sales proposal has several key purposes: 1) matches needs to benefits, 2) defines financial justification, and 3) reduces risk.

4

Understanding What to Include in a Buyer-Focused Proposal

Johnny decided to hold a brainstorming session with his team to improve their sales proposals and close ratios. He knew that their new proposal needed to be drastically better than the current model. He now realized that the first model he developed was just a document containing the price, product specs, and information about the company. He also realized that all the work he and his team had done on answering the question "Why would a company buy our products and services?" was going to help them design their new proposal—it was simply unconscious competence to have started that project!

Johnny didn't know what the new proposal was going to look like, but he did know that it was going to focus on the buyer and create compelling reasons for choosing his company's products. He also knew that when they got the content right, he probably needed to work on the proposal's appearance. But right now his goal was to develop the best proposal in the industry!

When you write a sales proposal, pretend you are having a private conversation with the buyer's decision makers. During the conversation, you tell them about critical issues that you see in their business, define their impact, and tell them what they need. Then describe how your product can offer solutions. And during your conversation you give them all the information that they need to make an informed buying decision.

If you don't give the buyer a proposal, you don't get to have the private conversation with the decision makers. This creates big problems. In the worst case, the buyer may not know exactly what you're selling and how it can reduce or avoid costs or increase revenues. In the best case, neglecting the proposal makes you appear indifferent or apathetic.

Using a one-size-fits-all, boilerplate proposal is better than not sending any proposal, but it doesn't work very well. With a boilerplate proposal, you're telling the buyer that it's exactly like all your other buyers—not a very stimulating conversation for the decision makers. Neither does using a *so-what* proposal—a proposal that doesn't provide the buyer with any financial justifications for making a change. This type of proposal does send a clear message to the decision makers: "You do the math, because I don't care or know how to do it myself."

Buyers are looking for detailed information that's addressed specifically to them—they need some input and help in making an important decision. In this chapter, I take you inside a proposal so that you can see exactly where its power comes from and so that you can avoid some common proposal mistakes.

Avoiding the Pitfalls: No Proposal, Boilerplate, and So-What Proposals

To better understand what to include in your proposal and the importance of your proposal development process, you need to learn what can happen if you:

- Don't write proposals
- Write *boilerplate* proposals
- Write *so-what* proposals

No proposal creates problems

Here are some occasions when you may be tempted to not write a proposal:

- Your contact at the buyer tells you that he can get the deal approved without a proposal.

- You've demonstrated your product to the decision makers and they were really impressed. No one asked for a proposal and you didn't ask if you needed to present one.

* You know it's going to take you two days to write a proposal and you just don't have the time. Besides, your contact has enough information from you and knows enough about your product to get the deal approved.

If you don't write a proposal, what does the buyer use to make a decision and what starts its decision process? Obviously the buyer can make a decision without a proposal, but there's not a clearly defined offer from you, the seller, other than price. Perhaps the decision makers won't feel any sense of urgency. More important, if they only have a price, maybe they will want another price or two—here comes the competition. Oh yeah, the final thing that could happen if you don't write a proposal when the buyer needs one: NO SALE.

Boilerplate proposals show lack of empathy

A *boilerplate* proposal is a proposal in which most of the wording is the same for all buyers. The only difference from one of the seller's proposals to the next is usually the buyer's name and the price. Boilerplate proposals send several bad messages to a buyer:

* **All buyers are the same.** The seller doesn't care that buyers have different business operations or unique business issues and needs.

* **The buyer is not a key account.** The buyer's business isn't that big of a deal for the seller.

* **The seller has untrained or perhaps inexperienced sales people.** The sales people haven't been trained or don't follow a consultative sales process and the seller's proposal development process is simple—just change the name and price and here's your proposal.

* **The seller is selling a commodity.** The seller's product is a just another commodity and the buyer should really only care about price and availability.

Believe it or not, some companies that sell very complex products only use boilerplate proposals. These sellers have reasons for doing so and they usually include one or more of the following. They want to:

* Deliver a standard sales message. Make sure all their sales professionals correctly describe generic product features or service capabilities.

* Make sure that each proposal contains some standardized wording that's needed to satisfy a legal or regulatory issue.

- Make it very easy for their sales professionals to get a proposal in the hands of a buyer—*we don't need no stinking proposal development process around here.*

Boilerplate proposals don't give a buyer any compelling reasons to make a change because they don't contain any buyer-specific information. A fancy brochure and a price quote serve the same purpose as a boilerplate proposal.

Here's a classic boilerplate proposal situation from a sales call we made several years ago. It's real and it concerns a large truck leasing company that used nothing but boilerplate proposals. Its excuse for this practice was that it wanted to make sure that all of its proposals completely described how it did business. Except for the buyer's name appearing wherever the word-processing system found the <<customer name>> field, the leasing company's proposals were really little more than long, boring brochures. And they weren't very well written. The proposals forced prospective buyers to figure out, on their own, how the leasing company's services and systems could improve the buyer's operations and reduce truck acquisition and operating costs.

The real irony is that this truck leasing company had one of the best and most sophisticated truck leasing services available—maybe the best in the country at that time. But the company's president said he wanted his sales professionals to rely on relationship selling—you know, lunches, dinners, golfing, and schmoozing with customers. He didn't care if their sales professionals were consultative and he really didn't put much value in the need for a buyer-focused sales proposal. He didn't seem to care that their boilerplate proposals failed to define a buyer-specific application and the resulting benefits. He felt the only thing his company's customers really cared about was price. Well, his company's boilerplate proposals helped buyers focus on that!

It's not surprising that this leasing company closed less than 25 percent of their deals. This meant its competitors, probably with lesser services and equivalent prices, won 75 percent of the time. It appears as though relationship selling wasn't enough to close more business. If relationship selling was as important as the president thought, then 75 percent of the company's prospects didn't like his sales professionals! Perhaps their relationships weren't very meaningful.

You may be thinking, "But if the truck leasing company can submit more proposals than the other companies, they don't need to have a real high success rate." True, but submitting more proposals means the sales force has to make more calls and schmooze more prospects. The cost for making sales calls continues to rise while most companies are trying to cut travel and entertainment budgets. So, the numbers game doesn't work too well in a complex sales situation.

Avoiding so-what proposals

A *so-what* proposal isn't much more effective than a boilerplate proposal. A so-what proposal doesn't give your buyer the financial justification that it needs to make a buy decision because your value proposition is deficient.

To decide if you're writing so-what proposals, ask your buyers what they think. Get their reactions to your proposals. Or, you know you're writing so-what proposals if a buyer makes one or more of the following statements:

* Your product seems like a good idea, but I just don't know what it'll do for our bottom line.

* Sounds great, but how will it in work in our business?

* I don't understand what's really in it for us.

In most cases, a person who says he doesn't understand how your product will benefit his business is also admitting you have failed to give him and his company's decision makers a document that helps them make an informed buying decision.

A so-what proposal lacks the application detail and financial justifications that your buyer's top management needs to make the buy decision. If your contact likes your product, he or she may try to develop financial justifications to support your proposal. But, you're better able to analyze the financial benefits of your product, rather than the buyer. Certainly you will know more about the application and financial benefits of your product than a prospective customer!

Following Commonsense Guidelines

Use common sense as you develop your sales proposals. Consider this section as a reminder of all the "obvious" things that you should keep in mind. The tips I give you here are the basis for the five-part proposal I show you later in this chapter and throughout this book.

Develop it from the buyer's viewpoint

When you develop a proposal, always try to put yourself on the buyer's side of the desk; pretend you're one of the buyer's decision makers. Look at your proposal from that viewpoint. If you had to make the buying decision, what would you:

* Expect the seller to know about your business?

* Need to know about the seller's proposed product?

* Want to know about the seller's company and how it does business?

Developing your proposals from the buyer's viewpoint may be the most important guideline in this book. Putting yourself in the reader's mind will quickly put your sales proposals on the top of the stack.

Give it order and make it flow

Your proposal should have a logical flow of information and ideas. For example, your proposal should include a description of the custom application of your product and then present the resulting features and benefits.

Your proposal also should group similar types of information. One main section of your proposal should contain all the information about your company. For example, you present all the things a buyer may want to know about your company and how you do business—your mission statement, company history, research and development programs, and so on—in one section.

Educate the reader

Try to write every proposal as if one of the decision makers had little or no knowledge about the specific business function or operation being discussed. For whatever reason, he doesn't know anything about this particular part of the buyer's business and the related improvement opportunity. In other words, don't assume that all of the decision makers have the same knowledge level. You will write a better proposal if you assume one decision maker doesn't know anything. Your proposal should give every one of its readers all the information they need to make an informed buying decision.

Control length

Everyone wonders about proposal length. Here are some of the most frequently asked questions on that subject:

- Can a proposal be too long?

- Should a $300,000 proposal be ten times longer than a $30,000 proposal?

- Will a buyer think that something's missing in a proposal if it's shorter than other proposals?

Part of the answer to questions about proposal length is that a complex product or critical business issues probably dictate a proposal that needs to be fairly lengthy. The cost of your proposed product also may affect a proposal's length (although a $300,000 proposal definitely does not need to be ten times longer than a $30,000 proposal). Another factor that affects your proposal's length is the amount of information it includes about your company to help a buyer decide if it wants to do business with you. Even issues like font size, white space, and page margins affect length.

The best answer to any question about how long or short a proposal should be may be this: your proposal should be long enough to get a signed contract, but short enough to hold the reader's attention. (Hey, that sounds like an answer from a politician.)

Use these two guidelines if you're still wondering about your proposal's length:

- Ask your buyer what it expects. Some companies don't like to receive and may not accept lengthy proposals. They may expect that the main body of the proposal will be 10 to15 pages long—but they may not have limits on the number and length of appendices.

- Try to limit the amount of detail in the main body of the proposal. Remember that a well-written sales proposal won't bore the reader (too much). Therefore, avoid lengthy product descriptions, specifications, or implementation task lists in the main body. Instead, summarize this stuff and put the details in appendices.

Structuring Your Proposals

The next few pages give you an overview of the five-section proposal that we recommend. We have used this structure to design proposal models for all types of products and services. As you read about each main section's contents, think about how the structure creates a logical flow of information and ideas. You can find out all the details in

Chapters 5 through 11. The section titles used in these figures and tables are generic. Each section also shows you how to use custom titles.

Note that the first section of the proposal is background information about the *buyer,* not the seller. Be honest. In the last proposal you wrote, did the first proposal section provide background information about your company? Your proposals should reflect two integrated processes: your consultative sales and proposal development processes. If you sell consultatively, you focus on your buyer and your proposals should have the same focus.

Table 4-1 introduces the proposal sections that we recommend and briefly describes the contents of each.

 Table 4-1 Five-Section Proposal Structure

Section	Title	Comments
1	Background Information	Everything you learned about your customer during your sales process. This section *"sets the stage"* for your proposed product.
2	Proposed Solution	Everything your customer needs to know about your proposed product: description, application, features, and value proposition.
3	Implementation	The how, who, and when about implementing your product.
4	Seller Profile	Things your customer wants to know about your company.
5	Business Consideration	All the boring but necessary business stuff.

Here's the logic for using these five sections in this order:

- First, the buyer wants to know that you know about its company and have identified viable business issues and needs, *Section 1.*

- Next, the buyer wants to learn about your proposed product, the application in its company, and the financial and non-financial benefits the buyer can expect, *Section 2.*

- If the buyer buys into the proposed product section of your proposal, it then wants to learn about how you plan to deliver on the contract, *Section 3*.

- If your proposal accomplishes the first three things, the buyer probably asks the following question: "Hey, who are these guys?" So, you next need to give the buyer some info about your company, *Section 4*.

- Finally, the buyer is ready to look at all the business stuff associated with the deal, *Section 5*.

Your proposals will require more than the five main sections to be complete. Table 4-2 lists some other important components that you should include. Chapters 10 and 11 explain each component in detail.

Table 4-2 Other Important Proposal Components

Component	Comments
Title Page	The cover page to your proposal that, if titled correctly, can help focus the reader's attention.
Executive Summary	A concise synopsis of the entire proposal; a proposal in miniature.
Table of Contents	A listing of the proposal's main sections and subsections with page numbers.
Appendices	Brochures, detailed schedules, preprinted materials, and so on; used to support information summarized or referenced in the main proposal sections.

Figure 4-1 illustrates the five-section proposal structure. A version of this illustration appears in the chapters that discuss the five sections. The recommended subsections are slowly added to the figure as you work your way through book.

Figure 4-1 The Five Section Proposal Structure
(with blank subsections)

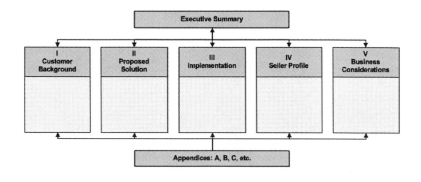

Stuff to Remember

Johnny and his team classified their current proposals as *so-what, boilerplate proposals*. They realized that in the past nobody had really thought much about structure, content, or flow of information. It was just cutting and pasting from several proposals and copying the buyer's logo onto the cover page. Johnny and his team knew they had to do better—a lot better.

√ Think of your sales proposal as having a private conversation with the buyer's decision makers in which you give them all the information that they need to make an informed buying decision.

√ If you don't write a proposal, the buyer has nothing on which to make a decision and nothing to start its decision process.

√ A *boilerplate* proposal uses wording that is the same for all buyers; it doesn't give a buyer any compelling reasons to make a change.

√ A *so-what* proposal doesn't give a buyer the financial justification to make a buy decision because the value proposition is deficient.

√ As you write a proposal, pretend you're one of the buyer's decision makers and decide what you need to know to make a decision.

√ Your proposal should have a logical flow of information and ideas.

5

Section 1: Writing First about the Buyer

At their first "Proposal Project" brainstorming session Johnny and his team agreed they should design their new proposal totally from the buyer's viewpoint. They wanted to start with a blank page. They also decided to act like they were the decision makers for the New Widget Corporation, a fictitious company. As decision makers, the first thing they were going to do was to identify what information they expect a seller should know about their company before they should propose purchase of the specific (their company's) product.

They agreed that as sellers their proposals first needed to demonstrate an understanding of the buyer's situation and the issues and needs that would compel a buyer to make a change. Unlike their old proposal that started with two pages of company hype, their new proposal was going to focus on the buyer.

Many sales professionals start their proposals with a background information section, but it's background about their company, not the buyer. What happened to putting the customer first? Some possible reasons for this flip-flop might be that the sales professional:

- Gets blank-page syndrome when he starts to write the proposal. Rather than stare at a blank screen, he writes about a subject he knows well—his company. After awhile, the creative juices start to flow and he includes some stuff about the buyer, but he buries it deep in his proposal.

- Thinks the buyer wants and needs to know a lot about his company (how big it is, how many offices it has, and so on) before getting into the real meat of the proposal, which is the buyer's critical business issues and how much money the buyer can make or save.

- Has always written proposals this way or he got a copy of a proposal from one of his peers and that's the way it was written, so it's okay.

Your proposal does need to include information about your company. But first focus your proposal on the buyer. Show the buyer that you understand its situation. This chapter explains how to get your proposal off to a great start—it's all about the buyer.

Sales and Proposal Development: Process Integration for Section One

The first section of the proposal contains lots of *process connections information* (PCI) and *common activities.* You might want to review Chapter 2 and Figure 2-1, which introduces these terms.

Certainly you can't develop a buyer-focused sales proposal without first gathering and defining buyer information. The first section of your proposal is where you'll put much of what you learn about the buyer. Figure 5-1 uses a variation of Figure 3-1 to highlight those sales tools, which are sources of PCI for section one. I use this graphical technique to help you identify the sales tools needed to gather buyer information for section one and all the other proposal sections.

These sales tools also help define the integrated activities or processes sales professionals will follow as part of their proposal development process. Obviously, some of these represent activities or process sales professionals also would use if selling consultatively. Therefore, they identify specific *common activities* when a seller integrates proposal development and consultative selling.

The toughest section to write

I think you'll find that the buyer background section of your proposal is the toughest section to write. It will require a thorough understanding of the buyer's situation, issues, and needs. You can only gain this information through conversations with the buyer in a consultative manner.

When I design proposal models for our clients, I see how some of their sales professionals struggle with the customer information requirements of this first section. A frequent comment expressed by some sales professionals is, "This is a lot of buyer information that we have to get." My standard reply is, "You're right, this is a lot of buyer information. What don't you need to know and I'll drop that from the proposal?" The typical response is, "Well, you're right, we should know all this about our buyers if we're giving them a proposal."

Figure 5-1 Sources of PCI Used in Section 1

Sales Tools	Process Connections Information									
	Background Information	Critical Business Issues, KPIs	Impacts on Business	Customer Stated Needs	Customer's Selection Criteria	Product/Service Application	Prices/Fees	Non-Financial Benefits	Financial Benefits	Implementation/Installation Variables
Customer Intelligence	S	S								
Customer's Web Site	S	S								
Prospect Survey	S	S		S	S					
Buyer Questionnaire	S	S	S	S	S					
KPI Input (Key Pain Indicator)	U	S		S						
Pricing/Configure System		U		U		S	S			S
ROI Valuation	U	S	S	S		U	U		S	
Sales Process Letters (various)	U	U	U	U	U	U	U	S	U	U
Sales Proposal	U	U	U	U	U	U	U	U	U	U

Showing that You Know Your Prospect

The first section of your sales proposal lets the buyer know what you know. The first section:

- Documents your in-depth understanding of your buyers and its critical business issues—those things you learned while you were face to face with the buyer's contact person, surfing the Internet, reading your buyer's annual report, and analyzing what you found.

- Provides detailed background information, including the key pain indicators (KPIs) that measure the buyer's critical business issue. You might find that some proposal recipients don't know as much as you may think they do about their own business.

- Sets the stage for the second section of the proposal, in which you roll out your product (or service).

You can't fake buyer knowledge and you obviously can't use boilerplate from other proposals while writing this section. It must demonstrate your thorough understanding of the buyer's business, particularly those functions that are relevant to the buyer's critical business issues.

Educating the Reader—Some Need Help

Use the background information section to educate the readers, the buyer's decision makers, by providing them with pertinent information about the critical business issues that their organization has. Give them the knowledge on which to base their buying decision. Equally important, make sure that all the buyer's decision makers have the same level of knowledge. If you do a good job with this section, you might impress the readers with how much you know about their company. The buyer may start to think you're more of a business consultant than a salesperson.

It's important to remember that decision makers want to know that you really understand their business. They also want to know that you've identified and clearly defined viable business issues for their company.

Even big guys can miss the point

Several years ago, a top-tier CPA firm gave me a proposal that it wanted me to evaluate using my Proposal RATER. They wanted to see if I could tell them whether the proposal was a winner or loser.

The CPA firm was proposing a $750,000 consulting engagement that would improve a defense contractor's manufacturing process by reducing its raw materials inventory levels. The proposal contained little information about the company's current manufacturing process and no quantitative data (key pain indicators) about the procurement process or its current inventory levels. The lack of customer information in the proposal gave me the impression that the CPA firm really didn't understand the problem. It seemed that either the CPA firm was unable to analyze the defense contractor's unique business situation or the CPA firm was proposing a major consulting engagement to correct a problem that it really didn't understand. Maybe it thought that its consultants would figure the problem out on the fly at the customer's cost.

This proposal was a loser. I suspect the manufacturing company's decision makers viewed the proposal much like I did. If the CPA firm had spent more time analyzing the defense contractor's situation, it may have been able to write a proposal that had some depth to it. The proposal needed a lot more background information about the defense contractor's procurement and manufacturing processes and current key pain indicators, including inventory volumes and costs. It also needed a clear critical business issue statement. With a bit more work, the CPA firm may have signed a nice, juicy $750,000 consulting contract.

Another thing that I'll always remember about this proposal was the appendix that contained ten or so biographical resumes of the partners and consultants that would be assigned to work on the project. Every resume was one-page long except one, which was two pages. The two-pager was much more expansive than the others. I asked my contact at the CPA firm if the person in charge of writing the proposal also had the inflated resume. Indeed he was. Interestingly, that person wasn't the partner-in-charge or even one of the managers.

Providing Unbiased Analyses: Just the Facts

Don't make the first proposal section your interpretation of the buyer's past bad decisions or poor management. Further, this section can't make it appear that the buyer isn't aware of some recent improvements or innovations in its industry.

One of the decision makers, or his or her boss or subordinate could be responsible for a current operational problem. You don't want to put something in your proposal that criticizes or embarrasses anyone reading your proposal. You could force a decision maker to defend his or her company's current situation (the problem), which could result in opposition to any change or buying decision that would improve the situation. Therefore, always adhere to the just-the-facts approach when you write the customer background section. Think about Joe Friday from Dragnet, "Just the facts, sir."

Picking a Title for the First Section

Picking a good title for your proposal's first main section is important. You can use one of these generic titles for section one:

- Current Situation

- Present Operations

- Background Information

If possible, try to select a section title that helps identify the problem or critical business issue available to your buyer. For example, rather than using the bland title "Current Situation," some sales professionals use these types of titles in their proposals:

- Current Equipment Maintenance Program Business Issues

- Customer Billing and EBPP Opportunities

You also can include the buyer's name in the section title to focus the reader's attention. Some examples:

- Acme Manufacturing: Equipment Maintenance Program

- 1st National Bank: Current Internet Banking Program

Deciding What Subsections to Include

Buyers and buying situations are unique; therefore, you must carefully decide what to include in the first section of your proposal. I recommend the following parts, and list them in the order that makes most sense:

- Buyer Background

- Current Operations or Functions

- Critical Business Issues

- Needs

- Purpose of This Proposal

Titling the Subsections

Table 5-1 provides some examples of subsection titles used by a software company selling electronic bill presentment and payment (EBPP) software.

Table 5-1 Examples of Generic and Specific Subsection Titles

Generic Title	Customer- or Buyer- Specific Title
Buyer Background	ABC Insurance Company: Background Information
Current Operations (or Functions)	Current Insurance Premium Billing Processes
Needs	ABC Insurance Company: EBPP Needs
Purpose of This Proposal	Purpose of This EBPP Proposal to ABC Insurance

Writing About the Buyer's Background

The customer background subsection in your proposal provides a brief overview of your buyer's business. Include general buyer information in this subsection—the type of information found in most annual reports or on a company's Web site. I'm talking about information like the number of employees, annual revenues, and the number of locations. Putting information like this in your proposal assures the buyer that you understand its business.

You can also use this subsection to include the detailed information that's relevant to the buyer's critical business issues and to your proposed product. For example, if you're trying to sell the buyer technical training for desktop applications, you probably should include which desktop applications the buyer currently uses and how many employees use them.

The following buyer background subsection examples can give you some ideas about how much detail to include in your buyer information subsection. Writing a buyer background section is easy. I wrote the following insurance example by taking information right from a Web site. Searching the Internet took us less than five minutes. I changed the company name and some of the information to protect the innocent.

AIS Background Information

The American Insurance Service Companies (AIS) have served the insurance, pension, and risk management needs of individuals and businesses for more than 120 years. Nearly 750 member cooperatives and associations own AIS's fiscal agent and parent company, American Insurance Service Cooperative. The AIS Companies include:

– American Service Casualty Insurance Company

– American Service Life Insurance Company

– AIS Service Insurance Company

– American Pension Solutions, Inc.

AIS has nearly 1,000 employees and exclusive sales representatives supporting the following core businesses:

– Commercial Insurance & Risk Management

– Personal Insurance & Risk Management

– Personal and Corporate Pension Solutions

Writing About Current Operations

Your proposal must clearly define the buyer's current operations as they relate to the critical business issues. In other words, write about that part of the buyer's business that can be changed by your proposed product. This subsection does the most to educate those decision makers who may have limited knowledge about one particular function in a large company. Remember that a winning sales proposal provides its readers with sufficient information about some aspect of the buyer's current situation to enable them to make an educated decision.

Use Key Pain Indicators to measure reality

This is where you really use the key pain indicators (KPIs). KPIs represent the variables that you and your buyer agree to use for measuring its current costs and revenues. Before you can calculate the financial benefits of your product for a buyer, you need to measure the *current* costs and revenues associated with its critical business issues. Use KPIs to do the measuring. When you calculate the *future* financial effects of your proposed product, use these same KPIs as a basis for your calculations.

For example, say that you're proposing a manufacturing company engage your executive recruiting firm for all its recruiting needs of employees at the middle-manager level and above. Obviously, your proposal needs to include information about the company's current management recruiting program. You may include

- The number of mid-level and senior managers in the company

- Current mid-level and senior manager recruiting practices

- Average annual turnover and retention rates for mid-level and senior managers

- The number of mid-level and senior managers hired each year

- Average salaries for mid-level and senior managers

- Average relocation costs for mid-level and senior managers

All of the items in the list are KPIs but the second. All the other items can be used to *measure* the costs of recruiting, hiring, and relocating a manager.

This subsection of your proposal should educate the buyer's decision makers about their company's current recruiting programs and challenges. More importantly, your proposal should reflect your in-depth understanding of the buyer's current mid-level and senior manager recruiting program. Certainly, the buyer's decision makers will feel more comfortable with your executive recruiting firm's capabilities when they see that your proposal presents this information.

Learning lots about your buyer's current operations and including this knowledge in your sales proposal can elevate your status in the buyer's eyes. Besides, knowing lots about a buyer's current operations and identifying viable business issues can make you seem less like another vendor and more like a business consultant. More importantly, knowing lots about how the buyer's operation works makes it easier to describe how your product will work in the buyer's business.

A proposal may not contain buyer-specific information for two possible reasons. The sales person:

- Knew the information but just didn't put it in the proposal

- Didn't know the information because his sales process wasn't consultative—perhaps he was just another peddler

Neither excuse is a good one!

In the following example, the seller is a software company selling an electronic bill presentment and payment (EBPP) system through which customer bills are presented and paid on the Internet. The software company uses the current operations section of its proposal to educate decision makers about the current cost of their company's paper-based billing operations.

As you read this next example, keep track of the key pain indicators that the software company is using.

Current Operations

The City of Westerville Public Utilities Department sends customer bills each month to residential, commercial, and industrial customers for water and sewer services. The following statistics define the scope and magnitude of the billing operation:

– Total commercial customers:	22,000
– Total residential customers:	108,000
– Total number of customers:	130,000
– Number of customers on auto draft:	5,000

The City of Westerville currently uses an IBM AS 400e RISC 9406-730 computer for its Customer Information System (CIS) and Cashiering System (CR). These systems are licensed from MuniSystems of Plano, Texas. The system is a DB2 proprietary database with SQL calls. Information can be exchanged using TCP/IP protocol.

BillDocs in Dallas, Texas, provides paper bill production and mailing services for the City of Westerville. BillDocs charges the city $0.825 for each bill mailed. This includes the cost for paper, envelopes, printing, and bulk mailing.

Westerville National Bank provides a retail lockbox service for the city. The bank receives and processes all payments sent by mail (approximately 96 percent of all bills). For each payment it processes, the bank charges the city $0.18. The bank provides payment information in machine-readable format, which is transmitted to the city on a daily basis.

If you were a decision maker reading this proposal, your interest would probably be piqued after you see exactly how much your company is currently paying to have its bills processed.

Writing About Critical Business Issues

The *critical business issues* are simply the opportunities that the buyer has to make or save money or avoid costs. You must accurately define critical business issues for the buyer and:

- Explain their impact on the buyer's business

- Define the costs that are now incurred that your product could cut or avoid or the new revenues that your product could help the company earn

The buyer must agree with you about the existence of the critical business issues and the validity of the financial measurements you use. You can't manufacture or engineer critical business issues for the buyer just to make a sale. If you do, you'll really seem like just another peddler to the buyer—doing whatever you have to in order to make a sale. Not only will you not make the sale, but your credibility will be shot.

If you've been methodical and thorough in gathering current operations data from the buyer, some aspect of the buyer's current operations will probably pop up like a red flag marking a critical business issue. I don't think that finding critical business issues is that difficult. The key is to know how your product can work in the buyer's business so that business issues you define help "set the stage" for your proposed product. Keep in mind that if you're selling a product that you know pretty well and understand how a business uses it to benefit its bottom line, you have a head start in identifying critical business issues.

For example, say that you're selling a data processing services system to Acme Manufacturing, a company that currently buys data processing services from a service bureau. You've listened carefully, taken good notes, and found that the $350,000 Acme is spending every year for data processing:

- Is 20 percent higher than what similar companies spend

- Represents 18 percent of Acme's "Other Expenses"— a big chunk

- Reduces the company's earnings per share by 4.3 cents

The numbers in the list are KPIs. KPIs are the variables that you and your buyer agree to use for measuring the buyer's current costs and revenues.

If you were proposing to sell Acme Manufacturing an in-house data processing system, you certainly should use these KPIs in the critical business issues subsection of your proposal. And you can and should use these numbers in the next main section of your proposal—the second section. In this section you describe your proposed solution and show how it will reduce the company's data processing costs and thereby increase earnings.

Five rules for creating effective critical business issues

In his book *ROI Selling,* Michael Nick defines five commonsense rules for creating effective business issues statements.

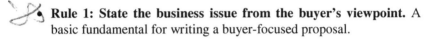

- **Rule 1: State the business issue from the buyer's viewpoint.** A basic fundamental for writing a buyer-focused proposal.

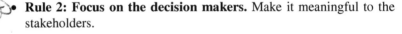

- **Rule 2: Focus on the decision makers.** Make it meaningful to the stakeholders.

- **Rule 3: Use the word *because*.** Here are some examples of *because* statements: *it takes too much time, it's too costly, there's a chance of missing.*

- **Rule 4: Phrase the business issue statement from the standpoint of a loss, and tie it specifically to a cost.**

- **Rule 5: The loss stated in your business issue statement should be measurable and quantifiable.** Measurable refers to the ability to "measure a result." Quantifiable refers to a numeric response.

Here's an example of a critical business issue statement Michael developed using these five rules:

Rule 1: ABC Software

Rule 2: wants to reduce its cost of sales

Rules 3 and 4: because the sales cycle is too long

Rule 5: and our costs continue to rise as the deals linger

Setting the stage for the proposed solution section

The critical business issue subsection of the first main proposal section is tied to the second section, in which you present your proposed solution. In the previous Acme Manufacturing example, if you were the sales professional for the in-house data processing vendor, your proposal needs to measure the financial benefits of your system based on Acme's KPIs—the Other Expenses and Earnings per Share measures. To do this, your proposal should include these KPIs in the first section and then should use them in the second section as a basis to calculate the financial benefits of your system.

Using this example, here's how your proposal should be designed so that the first section sets the stage for the second section.

Table 5-2   How Section 1 Sets the Stage for Section 2

If section 1 identifies the company's data processing cost . . .	Then section 2 should show how an in-house data processing system can . . .
Totals $350,000	Reduce that annual cost to less than $350,000
Is 20 percent higher than similar companies	Make this cost comparable to companies of similar size and type
Represents 18 percent of its "Other Expenses" budget line	Reduce data processing costs to less than 18 percent of the company's "Other Expenses"
Lowers its earnings per share by 4.3 cents	Lower earnings per share by less than 4.3 cents

When you analyze the financial benefits of your product in your sales proposal, keep in mind that most senior managers of corporations also own stock in the company. In the Acme example, assume the decision makers own lots of stock in the company. They will get excited when someone shows them how to reduce the impact of data processing costs on the company's earnings per share because it's money in their pockets. Using earnings per share as one of your key pain indicators sets the stage for a financial benefit calculation that shows how your proposed product can increase the buyer's earnings per share.

Writing About Buyer Needs

Your buyers have needs that are outgrowths of their critical business issues.

> **Need:** The fact or condition of not having enough; shortage; deficiency.

Buyers' decision makers must understand their company's available critical business issues and the financial and non-financial benefits provided by your product. Identifying the buyer's needs helps decision makers see the critical business issues and the financial benefits that are available.

Your critical business issue subsection begins to set the stage for introducing your product (the proposed solution) in the second section, and the needs subsection continues to set the stage. You first must clearly identify the buyer's *confirmed* needs. Just like you can't fabricate a buyer's critical business issue, you can't fabricate its needs. The buyer would perceive any fabrication as manipulative and not very reflective of a consultative selling process. You need to work closely with the buyer to help it define its needs. Your behavior should reflect your customer-focused consultative sales process.

Plan to spend some time working with your buyer to get its needs right. Be consultative. If you can understand and confirm the buyer's unique needs, you can use this knowledge to develop a custom application of your product. And your custom application can become the basis for converting your product's features into buyer-specific benefits—your *value proposition* for the buyer. (See the next chapter for more on value propositions.)

Identifying and defining the buyer's needs is really beneficial. Try this logic:

- **If** you can identify the buyer's needs, you can then define a unique product application for the buyer.

- **And** by defining a unique application, you present product features and resulting benefits that perfectly match (and satisfy) the buyer's needs.

- **Then** your proposal really can convince the decision makers that buying your product makes perfect sense.

It seems obvious that putting the buyer's needs in your proposal will help you close more business.

The following subsection example continues with the City of Westerville electronic bill presentment and payment (EBPP) case study. It follows along with the background information and critical business issues subsection examples found in this chapter.

The example below presents the needs the sales professional identified while working (selling consultatively) with representatives from the City of Westerville. In this example, Westerville's critical business issue is to offer EBPP to its customers. The critical business issue results in the needs listed in the following example.

This example shows how a proposal can contain some very specific buyer needs. After reading the example, you will read that the seller (the EBPP software vendor) has a program that will help the City of Westerville achieve each of its needs. The vendor's EBPP solution will be presented in the second section of the proposal. If you were a decision maker for the City of Westerville, would you be ready to see what the seller is going to propose?

City of Westerville: EBPP Needs

We identified the following electronic bill presentment and payment (EBPP) processing system needs for the City of Westerville during analysis of its current utility billing operations:

– Acquire an EBPP system or services to provide a dynamic, new service to utility customers and reduce paper-based costs.

– Begin offering EBPP services to Westerville utility customers during the 2nd quarter of 2008.

– Allow customers to self-activate EBPP services

– Allow customers to make payments by either charging their checking accounts or credit cards

– Provide customers with a 12-month rolling history of past bills and payments

– Expand EBPP services to other city services, e.g., property taxes and parking tickets.

Wrapping up the First Section by Explaining the Proposal's Purpose

You may think that if your first section effectively defines the buyer's critical business issues and needs, any reader will know why you're proposing a change. You may think that you don't need to explain the purpose of the proposal. Nevertheless, that's what I suggest you do at the end of the background information section—before you move on to propose a way to capitalize on what you have described as the buyer's critical business issues.

If you're seriously considering ignoring my advice, all I can say is this: Never overlook an opportunity to make sure that your proposal keeps the reader focused. This subsection is especially worthwhile if any of your buyer's decision makers have limited knowledge about the operation affected by the critical business issue.

The following example shows the kind of language that works in the wrap-up. ElectroBill is proposing to install its electronic bill presentment and payment (EBPP) software. This subsection helps carry the reader into the next section, where ElectroBill presents its proposed EBPP system.

Purpose of this Proposal

ElectroBill's proposal to the City of Westerville has two purposes:

1. Show how its EBPP system can:

    a. Provide a new service to the city's utility customers

    b. Reduce total billing costs

    c. Be used to bill and receive payments for other services

2. Present ElectroBill's proposed application of its EBPP system for Westerville and describe the resulting benefits.

Looking at Section One from the Buyer's Viewpoint

Decision makers carefully read the first proposal section to decide if you really understand their business and have accurately identified valid critical business issues for their company. Your buyer background information, particularly the buyer's KPIs, must be accurate and up to date. The defined critical business issues must be legitimate and the associated needs must reflect those identified and confirmed with your contact person during your consultative sales process.

If you skip steps or take shortcuts in your proposal development process, your lack of in-depth buyer knowledge can be very obvious in the first section of the proposal. You may find that as you write this section, some of the critical buyer information you need is missing. As a result, your proposal will lack depth. You can expect that most readers will immediately spot these deficiencies and may discount the rest of your proposal. The readers may think that if you can't make the effort to learn about their company and understand their unique situation, how can you possibly propose a product that can work for them?

Figure 5-2 Section 1 of the Five Section Proposal Structure

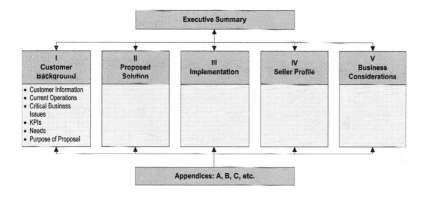

Stuff to Remember

Johnny's comment to the team after they completed the design of their proposal's first section was, "It's amazing how easy this is once you get the right viewpoint—*the buyer's.*" Everyone seemed to understand that a winning proposal had to be focused on the buyer. Their first proposal section contained buyer information that was relevant to purchase of their product. It certainly was going to let a buyer know that they understood its unique situation and had identified viable business issues and needs. Next, they were going to design the section that would propose the solution.

√ You should constantly ask one question when writing a buyer background section for your proposal: *If I had to approve this purchase, does this section provide me with enough background information about the current situation to understand the need for a change?*

√ Get all the decision makers' knowledge levels to the point where they understand the current situation and the critical business issues that you've identified for their company. Always give them sufficient information so that they feel confident making a critical buying decision.

√ Think about this logic when you're selling and writing a proposal. If, after reading your proposal, the decision makers don't understand their current situation, they probably won't understand the critical business issues facing their company. And if they don't understand their critical business issues, they probably won't buy your proposed solution.

√ Make sure that the buyer's decision makers can easily understand that their company has an opportunity to reduce or avoid costs or increase revenues. Keep the decision makers in mind as you write this section of the proposal.

6

Section 2: Proposing Business Solutions to Your Customer

After their first "Proposal Project" brainstorming session, Johnny and his team knew taking the roles of decision makers for the New Widget Corporation gave them the perfect perspective for designing their new proposal model—the buyer's. The "Buyer Information" section they had designed was really buyer-focused. They realized that the buyer information–gathering activities of their new "Proposal Development Process" were going to make them behave more like consultants and less like salespeople. One of the team members said, "Hey, that's a description for consultative selling."

The team had decided the second main section of their proposal should be used to present their proposed solution. Since the first section described the buyer's current situation, business issues, and needs, it seemed logical to use the next section to describe their product and explain how and why it was a sound business decision to buy it. They put on their New Widget Corporation decision-maker caps and went to work. They wanted to continue the buyer-focused theme for the proposed solution section of their new model.

After the first main sales proposal section, the next most difficult to write is the second section. This is where you tell your prospective customer how it can solve its business problems by purchasing your product. We don't mean solving *all* its problems, just those associated with the critical business issues you have noted in the first section. If you want to convert the buyer's business issues into sales, you have to describe in your proposal how your product can resolve them.

If you do a good job writing about your proposed solution, you can really set yourself apart from the competition. But you must provide the buyer's decision makers with a clear understanding of your proposed product, making sure to thoroughly describe how your product will help the buyer resolve its critical business issues identified in the first section of your proposal.

Remember that the first section of your proposal should *set the stage* for your proposed solution. In the second section, you explain the proposed solution by showing a realistic application of your product in the buyer's business. This puts you one step closer to closing the deal and getting the big commission check.

Linking the First and Second Sections

As I discuss in Chapter 1, we believe strongly in *consultative* selling. If you have the right and accurate information about the buyer's business and operations in section one of your proposals, then you have a strong foundation for writing a winning section two. These two sections link together and help the buyer make an informed buying decision. Specifically, your proposal's first and second sections link the buyer's:

- Critical business issues with the application of your product
- Needs to your product's features and the resulting benefits

To show you how a buyer's critical business issues and needs link to a seller's product application, features, and benefits, take a look at the following example. It shows the notes a salesperson from *ePayroll Services* made after a call on *Union Data Services*. Union Data Services is in the market for an electronic payroll service. The first example represents the buyer background information section (section one) of the proposal.

ePayroll Services is going to be able to make clear connections between its product and the Union Data Services' critical business issue and the resulting needs.

Union Data Services: Current Payroll Situation

Union Data Services (UDS) provides custom data processing services to 85 cooperative utility companies in six states. Its corporate headquarters is in Madison, Wisconsin, and it has four regional offices in the Midwest. The company has rapidly grown since its formation in 2001 from 15 employees to 500 at the end of 2007.

UDS has outgrown its current, off-the-shelf payroll system because it is experiencing high processing costs and expensive posting delays from its job reporting system.

During our analysis, we identified the following payroll processing needs for UDS:

- Lower payroll processing costs.
- Integrate the payroll system with the company's job reporting system.
- Provide online input from its main office and four regional sites.
- Satisfy all tax and regulatory requirements.
- Offer direct deposit as an employee option.

Process Integration for Section Two

The second section of the proposal also contains lots of *process connections information* (PCI) and *common activities.* You might want to review Chapter 2 and Figure 2-1, which introduce these terms.

You can't develop a buyer-focused sales proposal without using the buyer information contained in the first section as a basis for proposing a solution. Further, the proposed solution section will use some of the buyer information to justify the purchase and explain why buying your product makes good business sense. The second section of your proposal is where you define the application of your product and its value proposition for the buyer. Figure 6-1 uses a variation of Figure 3-1 to highlight those sales tools, which are sources of PCI for section two.

These sales tools also help define the related activities sales professionals will follow as part of their proposal development process. Obviously, some of these represent activities sales professionals also would use if selling consultatively. Therefore, they identify specific *common activities* when a seller integrates consultative selling and proposal development.

Figure 6-1 Sources of PCI Used in Section 2

Sales Tools	Background Information	Critical Business Issues, KPIs	Impacts on Business	Customer Stated Needs	Customer's Selection Criteria	Product/Service Application	Prices/Fees	Non-Financial Benefits	Financial Benefits	Implementation/ Installation Variables
Customer Intelligence	S	S								
Customer's Web Site	S	S								
Prospect Survey	S	S		S	S					
Buyer Questionnaire	S	S	S	S	S					
KPI Input (key pain indicator)	U	S		S						
Pricing/Configure System		U		U		S	S			S
ROI Valuation	U	S	S	S		U	U		S	
Sales Process Letters (various	U	U	U	U	U	U	U	S	U	U
Sales Proposal	U	U	U	U	U	**U**	**U**	**U**	**U**	U

Picking a Title for the Second Section

Here are some plain-vanilla choices for the title of the main section of your proposal where you present proposed solutions to the buyer:

- Proposed Services
- Proposed Project
- Proposed Solutions

- Proposed Consulting Engagement

- Proposed Strategy

You're probably better off if you can come up with a section two title that mentions the name of the proposed solution or describes the solution. For example, a financial asset management company might title the second section *Proposed Personal Financial Management Services.* A software company could use the name of its proposed system in the section title, such as *Proposed PowerMfg System.*

Deciding What Subsections to Include

I recommend four subsections for section two:

- Product description

- Product application

- Non-financial (qualitative) benefits

- Financial (quantitative) benefits

Remember, I use *product* to mean either a product or a service. If you are selling a service, your first two sections would cover the service description and the service application.

Note: I list non-financial benefits before financial, but you can change the order if you want. Some companies like to present financial benefits first. Others reverse the order. If you can't decide, ask the buyer what it prefers.

Titling the Subsections

You can also use subsection titles that include the name of the proposed product. For example, ePayroll Services sells PayDay, a payroll processing service. The seller can apply the title as shown in Table 6-1. Using the buyer's name in the subsection titles makes it pretty obvious to the reader that the subsection describes the application of the payroll service in the reader's company.

Table 6-1   Examples of Generic and Specific Subsection Titles

---

Generic Title	Customer- or Buyer-Specific Title
Product Description	PayDay: Overview
Product Application	PayDay for Union Data Services
Non-Financial Benefits	PayDay: Non-Financial Benefits
Financial Benefits	PayDay: Financial Benefits

Describing Your Product

The product description subsection must give the buyer a general idea of what your product is all about. Follow these guidelines:

- Tell the buyer exactly what you want it to do with your product. There's nothing wrong with making sure the buyer's decision makers are on the same wavelength that you are.
- Describe the product.
- Describe optional product components.

This one-sentence example leaves absolutely no doubt about what the seller wants the buyer to do.

> ePayroll Services (EPS) proposes that Union Data Services convert its internal payroll processing and systems to the EPS PayDay payroll service.

Describing the Standard Product

Give the buyer a crisp, concise description of your proposed product. Writing this description should be easy. You can probably get most of the information you need from one of your own brochures or right off your company's Web site. Be careful to include information that you would want to know if you had to make the buying decision. Your description can include such things as operating specifications, capacities, service levels, service frequency, deliverables, and so on.

Describing Options

If your product has options, tell the buyer about them even if those options are not part of the proposed application. Identifying options lets the buyer know that they're available.

Some of my clients don't want to include any information about options in their product description subsection. They worry that listing options can confuse the buyer, and that's a valid concern. But if you think of this part of your proposal as a brochure, you can use it to let the buyer know about everything that's available with your product. I also think listing options can lead to future sales. Maybe one of the decision makers will see an option she likes and add it to the deal! See Figure 6-2 for an example of a product description subsection.

Pretend you're a decision maker at Union Data Services. Does the service description you see in the following example give you enough information to help you understand EPS's payroll processing services?

Proposed PayDay Services™

ePayroll Services (EPS) proposes that Union Data Services convert its internal payroll processing system to the EPS PayDay payroll services.

EPS provides payroll processing services that include:

- Training Union Data Services payroll specialist to perform payroll-related responsibilities
- Calculating payroll and federal and state tax liabilities
- Posting payroll data to general ledger
- Monitoring payroll tax deposit due dates and sending advisory email messages
- Monitoring changes in federal and state payroll tax laws
- Preparing and filing payroll tax returns including the preparation of W-2s

EPS offers these options:

- **PayDay Connect:** EPS's Web-based entry system allows payroll specialist a secure, convenient, easy, and accurate way to complete all payroll entry and maintenance functions.
- **Direct PayCheck:** Electronic employee payroll deposits to any financial institution in the United States.
- **TaxPay:** Automatic preparation, filing, and payment of federal, state, and local payroll taxes.

The description of your product should be no longer than is necessary to deal with the complexity of your product. Keep in mind that you're writing a business proposal, not a technical proposal. Make sure that the technical content of this subsection doesn't overshadow the business aspects of your proposed solution. Where possible, summarize the technical information and use a supporting appendix for the details.

Covering Application Details

Always use the second subsection in section two to describe the buyer-specific application of your proposed product. Give the buyer a very specific explanation of how your product can work in its business. Keep in mind that if your product description subsection (which comes right before this subsection) is well written, writing this subsection should be easy. Consider following these guidelines when you write an application subsection:

- Start by telling the buyer what's going to happen.

- Continue by explaining how your product can work in the buyer's business, including how any proposed options can work.

Telling Them What's Going to Happen

In one or two paragraphs, explain how you plan to install or implement the proposed product in the buyer's business. This explanation doesn't need to describe your implementation methods or schedule in detail (you can do that in the next proposal section—the third section). Rather, tell the buyer more about how and when you're going to install, convert, deliver, or implement the product.

Here is a very good short explanation of how a product will be applied to a buyer's business:

> The American Institute on Substance Abuse in the Workplace (AISAW) will implement its OnAlert program at all Pacific Food Systems (PFS). AISAW staff will:
>
> - Conduct all training and rollout sessions
> - Provide quarterly program audits and management reports

Explaining the Application

Tell readers exactly how your product can work for them. Remember that the proposal recipient has just finished reading a description of your product in the previous subsection. So, you don't need to repeat product description information in the application subsection. Simply tell the buyer how your product can work in its unique business environment by:

- Highlighting key product components and describing how each works

- Describing which product options will be used and how they work

Advantages of Separating the Description and Application

You may think that combining the description and application subsections would be easy. Doing so can certainly cut a few pages out of your proposal, which means the buyer has less to read. In some situations and for some products, combining these two subsections makes sense. So, if you think doing so can work for your company, give it a try. However, having separate description and application subsections has some real advantages.

- You only have to write the description subsection one time and you only have to rewrite it when your product offering changes. Otherwise, you can treat it as part of your proposal model's standard wording.

- A separate description subsection gives you the opportunity to identify optional product components. As previously mentioned, putting product options in your proposals lets the buyer know what options are available (the application subsection tells the buyer which options have been selected for it).

- A separate application subsection is shorter than a subsection that combines the description and application. A separate application subsection is also easier for you to write and easier for the buyer to read than a combined section.

- If you ever plan to automate proposal production, doing so is much easier if you use separate product description and application subsections. The description subsection will be part of your proposal model, that's the same for all buyers. The application subsection will vary from buyer to buyer.

Answering the Buyer's Question: "What's in it for Us?"

In addition to describing your product and explaining its application, the second section of your sales proposal shows how your product benefits the prospective buyer. Benefits can be either *non-financial* or *financial:*

- **Non-financial** (or *qualitative*) benefits are hard to measure in dollars and cents (guess that explains the name). These benefits represent *soft value* rather than the *hard value* provided by financial benefits. For example, "Gives students real-time feedback to measure progress" is a non-financial benefit of computer-based training (CBT). The buyer and the seller know this is a very real benefit of CBT, but trying to measure this benefit in dollars and cents makes no sense.

- **Financial** (or *quantitative*) benefits represent the reduced or avoided costs or increased revenues provided by your product. Your proposal should calculate the buyer's financial benefits using the buyer's key pain indicators as a basis for the calculation. For example, "Eliminates student travel costs" is a financial benefit of computer-based training (CBT). If you were selling CBT, one of the financial benefits in your proposal would calculate exactly how much money the buyer can save by not sending students (in this case, the buyer's employees) out of town for training.

Delivering Value through Benefits

As you can imagine, the non-financial and financial benefits of your product are important to the buyer. They represent the *value proposition*. Some use the terms *value-adding* or *value justification*.

The two benefits subsections of your proposal are much more convincing if you've done your job as a sales professional. To develop buyer-specific benefits—the value proposition—some of your proposal development and consultative sales process activities, the *common activities,* must:

- Identify the buyer's key pain indicators and needs

- Figure out how your proposed product can work in the buyer's unique environment—the application

These sales activities typically present the greatest challenges in complex sales situations and the proposal development process. The good news is that if you do a thorough job of selling and developing the first parts of your proposal well, coming up with the value proposition should be fairly simple.

Using benefits to duplicate success

One of my clients is a printing and duplication company. It wanted to provide printing and outsourcing services to a private university in southern Wisconsin. To develop buyer-specific non-financial and financial benefits, its sales professional and proposal team analyzed the university's printing and duplication functions. They looked at such things as current costs, staffing and equipment, job types, volumes, and future projections. They also identified the university's printing and duplication needs and objectives. Of course, these were the consultative selling activities that were vital to writing the buyer background section of the proposal.

After the printing and duplication company understood the university's situation, it easily formulated a unique outsourcing service plan. Having a custom application made defining buyer-specific financial and non-financial benefits easy. And the benefits offered compelling reasons for the university to outsource these services. To the university's decision makers, the application and benefits subsection in the proposal made it seem as though the printing and duplication company had designed its outsourcing services just for their university.

Users Like Non-financial Benefits More Than Decision Makers Do

The end-users of your product are probably more interested in its non-financial benefits than the decision makers are. End-users are much closer to the real action and they're the ones who actually will use your proposed product. Therefore, end-users more clearly understand how your product can improve operations. The decision makers, of course, are usually more interested in the monetary benefits—probably because their bonuses are tied to how much money the company makes.

Generic Benefits Are Less Effective

A winning proposal must go beyond generic benefits statements. Here's a generic statement:

> "Automated document assembly can save your staff valuable time."

That statement has little meaning to end-users or decision makers. These end-users and decision makers may not understand which company documents need to be automated and how automating assembly can save time.

You can make that generic statement into a buyer-specific one:

> "Automated document assembly of all annuity plan agreements will eliminate clerical errors."

This means something to a user reading the proposal who manages the clerical staff that physically produces the annuity plan agreements for the company. This benefit is also meaningful to a decision maker who may be thinking that the company can cut clerical staff if, by implementing the system, the company will have fewer errors assembling annuity plan agreements—decision makers are always thinking about money!

Benefits Spring from Product Features

When you only describe the *features* of your product you sound like a talking data sheet or brochure. When you describe the *benefits* that your product delivers, you're talking to the buyer because buyers don't buy features they buy the benefits provided by the features. Here are some examples:

- Consumers don't buy fuel-efficient cars; they buy economy.
- Companies don't buy video surveillance and access control systems; they buy safety and security for their customers and employees.
- Companies don't buy corporate jet aircraft; they buy convenience for their executives to travel whenever they need without the hassles of airport security.

Follow these steps to translate features into benefits:

1. List a product feature.
2. Select an "action verb," such as offers, allows, reduces, etc.
3. State the benefit.

For example, our fictitious company, ePayroll Services (EPS), sells payroll processing systems to small- to medium-sized organizations. EPS developed generic non-financial benefits based on two capabilities: remote data entry and direct deposit of paychecks to employee accounts. Table 6-2 shows how an EPS sales professional used these generic benefits to develop buyer-specific non-financial benefits for Union Data Services (UDS).

The column on the left is standard product-feature language—the kind of language you expect to see in sales literature. The middle column moves a big step closer to the buyer by introducing the human element. The column on the right tells exactly how *this* buyer will benefit.

Table 6-2   Feature to Benefit Conversion Examples

Feature (or Capability)	Generic Benefits	Buyer-Specific Benefit
Romote data entry of payroll information via secure Internet connection	Allows data ontry clerks with Internet access to Input payroll information from any location.	Allows UDS payroll clerks to input payroll information from Its headquarters and four Midwest locations.
		Eliminates the need for UDS to load software on the desktop computers in its payroll offices to input to the EPS system.
Direct PayCheck— direct deposit of payroll checks	Requires UDS employees simply to have a checking or savings account at any financial institution.	Gives UDS the ability to add direct deposit to Its employee benefits.
		Reduces the amount of time needed to reconcile the UDS payroll account.

The custom benefits in Table 6-2 apply specifically to Union Data Service's unique situation. The EPS sales professional couldn't have developed these buyer-specific qualitative benefits if she didn't have an in-depth knowledge of Union Data's current data processing situation and a concise understanding of the proposed EPS payroll service application at Union Data.

Writing Financial Benefits

To a buyer, a financial benefit means either less or avoided costs or more revenue. Financial benefits are measured in dollars and cents. Use the financial benefits subsection of your proposal to show how your product reduces or avoids costs or increases revenues—in other words, how it lets the company resolve its business issues and satisfy its needs.

Make the financial benefits realistic and accurate and support them with an easy-to-understand, unquestionable financial analysis. Obviously, the content and accuracy of your financial benefits subsection is dependent on what you know about the buyer's business, including the buyer's key pain indicators that you identified in section one of the proposal.

Understanding key pain indicators is crucial to writing an effective financial benefits section. Remember; use the buyer's key pain indicators to measure its current costs, revenues, profitability, margins, productivity, or proficiency levels.

Here's an extended example of the financial benefits developed by my company, SalesProposals.com (SPC). I design, develop, integrate, and automate production of sales proposals for companies. Our automated system, Sales Document Builder (SDB), is Web-based and is available as software as a service (SaaS) or it can be licensed. The example shows the financial benefits a fictitious company, the Wellstone Corporation (WC), would realize if it developed custom proposal models for its sales professionals and their automated production using SDB.

Table 6-3 illustrates how our company (SalesProposals.com) works with buyers during our proposal development process. It lists:

- Key pain indicators one of our sales professionals would need to develop the financial benefits subsection

- Questions he or she may ask the prospective buyer to get values for the key pain indicators

- Answers the prospective buyer might give our sales professional

Table 6-3   Determining Key Pain Indicators

This is a Key Pain Indicator for the buyer	Our sales professional asks this question	The buyer might answer
Number of sales professionals	How many sales professionals work for your company?	30
Average fully loaded salary	What is the average salary and benefits for a sales professional?	$100,000
Number of sales managers	How many sales managers?	4
Average value of a proposal	What's the average dollar value of a proposal?	$250,000
Number of proposals written annually	How many proposals are written each year?	550
Number of proposals won annually	How many proposals are won each year?	140
Time to manually write a sales proposal	How long does it take a sales professional to write a proposal?	3 hours

Our sales professionals include the information in the above table plus additional calculated key pain indicators in section one of their proposals.

We defined some key performance indicators for Wellstone Corporation's current sales and proposal development processes:

- Number of sales professionals: 30
- Number of proposals written annually: 540
- Average proposal dollar value: $250,000
- Number of proposals closed annually: 140
- Current proposal close ratio: 25.43%
- Estimated average time needed to
  write a proposal: 3 hours
- Estimated average cost to write one
  proposal: $150

By getting these key pain indicators, our sales professionals are also able to develop solid financial benefits for the Wellstone Corporation in the second section of the proposal. The financial benefits cost-justify two things:

- The design and development of custom proposal models

- The implementation of Sales Document Builder as a service (SaaS) to automate proposal production for the WC sales professionals

Using past experiences with similar clients, we estimate that the custom proposal models we design will help Wellstone Corporation sales professionals close more business. We made the following estimates:

- WC's proposal close ratio will increase from the current 25.43 percent to 27.50 percent, which results in an increase in revenues of more than $2.8 million.

- Using Sales Document Builder will reduce individual proposal production times from three hours to forty-five minutes.

- We estimate our consulting fees and travel expenses will total $15,000.

The following example shows how our sales professionals use the key pain indicators and our estimates, to develop a financial benefits section in their proposals.

Financial Benefits for the Wellstone Corporation

Introducing the sales proposal models designed by SalesProposals.com and implementing Sales Document Builder (SDB) will enable Wellstone Corporation immediately to boost the profitability of its organization by:

- Reducing the time needed to produce custom sales proposals by using Sales Document Builder

- Increasing the company's Proposal Close Ratio through the introduction of new, buyer-focused sales proposal models that integrate into a consultative sales process

Cost-Benefit Analysis: Reduce Production Costs

• Annual current proposal writing costs		$82,500
• SDB Startup Fees	$2,000	
• Annual Sales Professional proposal writing costs using SDB	20,625	
• Annual SDB Fees	19,680	
• Total annual SDB proposal generation costs		<u>42,305</u>
• Total annual savings with SDB		**$ 40,195**
1st Year Return on Investment: Due to Reduced Production Costs		**95%**

Cost-Benefit Analysis: Increased Proposal Close Ratio

SPC Consulting Fees + Travel Expenses		$15,000
• Revenue generated from won proposals (current)	$35,000,000	
• Revenue generated from won SDB proposals	<u>37,812,500</u>	
• Increased 1st year revenues due to new proposal models		**$2,812,500**
1st Year Return on Investment: Due to Increased Proposal Close Ratio		**18,750%**

This financial analysis gives the Wellstone Corporations decision makers some good information on which to make an informed buying decision.

* The first-year savings in proposal writing costs are over $40,000 and the first-year ROI for using an automate proposal production system is 95 percent.

* The first-year increased revenues for writing winning, buyer-focused sales proposals are over $2.8 million and the first-year ROI using the new models is a whopping 18,750 percent.

It's always amazing to see the impact on revenue of more buyer-focused proposal models. Obviously the increased revenues result from a tighter integration of the proposals into a consultative sales process and a solid proposal development process. Sales professionals ask better questions and write proposals that help their prospective buyers make more informed buying decisions. The incremental costs to realize the higher revenues are low—virtually the same resources are now producing more.

Using Common Financial Benefit Calculations

Your sales proposal should calculate financial benefits using a method that the buyer's decision makers understand—probably a financial calculation that they normally use to make buying decisions. Ask the buyer how it wants to see financial benefits calculated in your proposal.

Two commonly used calculations for measuring the financial benefits of an investment are:

* Return on investment (ROI)

* The payback method

ROI is a very common investment performance measurement. It's calculated as follows:

Income (or savings) ÷ invested capital = return on investment

Here's the ROI calculation using the numbers from the New Wellstone Corporation (NWC) and our Sales Document Builder system to automate proposal production. In the first year, NWC would save $40,195 in sales proposal production costs by implementing Sales Document Builder. Its first year *return on investment* would be 95 percent.

$$\$40,195 \div \$42,305 = 95 \text{ percent}$$

The payback method calculates the period needed for the after-tax cash inflows from the product to accumulate to an amount equal to the capital invested in the product. In other words, it calculates how much time the product needs to pay for itself.

Invested capital ÷ annual after-tax cash inflow = payback period

Again using the numbers from the NWC and our example, the payback calculations are as follows, using a 20 percent tax rate for NWC. NWC would invest $15,000 in SalesProposals.com consulting services (including travel expenses) to increase its *Proposal Close Ratio* from 25.43 to 27.50 percent, which results in increased revenues of $2,812,500. Since the $2,812,500 is a before tax number, the sales professional needs to reduce it by the 20 percent tax rate (by a total of $562,000) to get a true payback period.

So $15,000 is the invested capital, which is divided by the first-year, after-tax revenue increase of $2,250,500. This calculation results in a payback period of 0.007 years—about two days!!!!

Figure 6-2 Sections 1 & 2 of the Five Section Proposal Structure

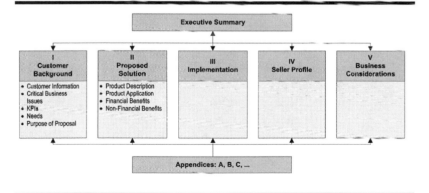

Stuff to Remember

The team asked Lee Ferguson, the company's chief financial officer, to teach how to develop ROI calculations for their new proposal model. Lee was surprised and flattered by the request. In a few hours, he developed a solid ROI calculation for the sales team, explained the basis for the calculations, and even developed a Microsoft Excel tool that they could use to work with their prospects. Johnny knew this new proposal model was going to raise the professionalism of his sales team.

√ Decision makers want to know something about what you're trying to sell, but they don't need a user's manual. Resist the temptation to load up this part of the proposal with your boilerplate materials. Remember that you can always put a data sheet or brochure in an appendix if you want the readers to have more information.

√ Most decision makers are more interested in the value proposition—how your product can improve their operations—than in the details of your product. They just need a brief explanation of how it will work.

√ The more you learn about developing winning proposals, the more you realize that there're no substitute for having lots of information about the buyer and solid product application knowledge.

√ Write the non-financial benefits subsection as if you were explaining the product's features to a new employee in the department that will use the product.

√ Buyer-specific benefit statements help the buyer understand the value provided by your product. Expect to use a combination of generic and buyer-specific benefit statements in your proposals—*don't only use generic statements.*

√ Spend some time trying to figure out exactly how your product features convert into buyer-specific benefits. Work with the buyer and be consultative.

7

Section 3: Explaining How You'll Implement the Solution

Johnny told his team they were on a roll. They had developed a solid proposed solution section for their model. As decision makers for the New Widget Corporation (a fictitious company), they thought their second section contained everything one needed—the proposed product, its custom application for the buyer, and a solid value proposition.

Now the team was in a quandary. What comes next—the proposal, information about the selling company, pricing detail, case studies, implementation information, or product data sheets? After some lengthy discussions and brainstorming, they reached a consensus—as decision makers they wanted to know how the seller was going to implement the product. After all, they had just decided to make a big investment. Now they wanted to know how the seller was going to deliver.

The team decided that they didn't know much about how their company's professional services staff and techies who installed the product. Some team members remembered implementation had briefly been discussed during the weeklong product training sessions that they all attended. But that was months ago for most. Besides, as sales professionals, they really did not pay that much attention to the topic. Now they knew they needed some help. Johnny decided he would invite the manager of professional services and one of the senior product managers to the next session. He told them to bring along all the information they had about how they managed implementation projects.

While reading your sales proposal, a decision maker who doesn't know much about your company or who isn't a current customer may start thinking:

> *Hey, this proposal really makes good sense. We can really help our bottom line with this proposed solution. But, can these guys deliver?*

A question like this one needs to be answered with the right information in your proposal. If you have been following the recommendations in this book, your proposal identifies the buyer's critical business issues and needs and then explains how your product represents a sound business decision. Suppose that the buyer really likes your proposal up to this point, but now the buyer senses some potential risks attached to choosing your company. So, when and how do you address those risks and raise the buyer's comfort level?

The time and place where you take the initiative is the middle section of your sales proposal—part three of the five-part proposal that I recommend in this book. You'll use this third section carefully to explain how you intend to implement the proposed project. This chapter shows how.

Sales and Proposal Development: Process Integration for Section Three

The third section of the proposal doesn't contain as much *process connections information* (PCI) as the first two sections. Consequently, there aren't as many *common activities* needed to develop this section. Note that you might want to review Chapter 2 and Figure 2-1, which introduce these terms.

You can't develop the implementation section of a buyer-focused sales proposal without first understanding the custom application of your product in the buyer's business. If you understand the application, then you also gain an understanding of how you will implement it for the buyer. Figure 7-1 uses a variation of Figure 3-1 to highlight those sales tools, which are sources of PCI for section three.

Figure 7-1 Sources of PCI Used in Section 3

Sales Tools	Background Information	Critical Business Issues, KPIs	Impacts on Business	Customer Stated Needs	Customer's Selection Criteria	Product/Service Application	Prices/Fees	Non-Financial Benefits	Financial Benefits	Implementation/ Installation Variables
Customer Intelligence	S	S								
Customer's Web Site	S	S								
Prospect Survey	S	S		S	S					
Buyer Questionnaire	S	S	S	S	S					
KPI Input (Key Pain Indicator)	U	S		S						
Pricing/Configure System		U		U		**S**	S			**S**
ROI Valuation	U	S	S	S			U	U		S
Sales Process Letters (various	U	U	U	U	U	U	U	S	U	U
Sales Proposal	U	U	U	U	U	**U**	U	U	U	**U**

Reassuring the Buyer

One of the functions of the third section in your proposal is to reassure the buyer. When a company decides to make a change by buying your product, the decision makers feel some risk. Pretend you're the CFO of a large manufacturing company and your company has decided to implement an enterprise resource planning (ERP) system. Implementing this type of system is a big deal for any company. As you review the proposals from the system vendors, you start to feel the risk associated with this big, critical decision. You feel two types of risk:

- **Business risk.** If you make the wrong choice, you create problems for the company, which can result in lost revenues or higher production costs. Profits could head south. You know that if profits are down, the board of directors will start pressuring the president. And, the president will probably want to try another reorganization to deflect the heat.

- **Personal risk.** A wrong decision reflects on you personally. Since you're the CFO, the other decision makers think you know lots about these types of systems, even though you're not an expert. So, they look to you to really study the options and recommend an ERP system that makes the most sense for the company. If you pick the wrong system, your name will be tied to any problems that result from the choice. You know that if the integration bombs, it's *your* system.

As a salesperson, you can reduce the risk that the CFO in the ERP system example feels. First, you can reassure the CFO that you've thoroughly studied his company's operations. You do this in section one of your proposals. Then, you define how your system can work in the CFO's company—section two of your proposal. In the third section you convince the CFO that your company can really deliver by presenting your implementation plans.

Note that you also use customer references to reassure the buyer, as I write about in the next chapter.

Using the Implementation Section to Show You've *Been There, Done That!*

This section of your proposal should describe your company's standard implementation methods, project management techniques, or business practices. It should define the steps, phases, and activities that your company normally follows. It should also identify the resources your company will use to implement your proposed product. It should also include an estimated schedule for completing the implementation.

This section can send the buyer one strong signal about your company's ability to deliver on the contract—*been there, done that!* In other words, after reading your proposal's implementation section, the buyer should realize that your company has experience in successfully implementing its products.

If your company is brand new or if this is your first project as an independent consultant, you can still give the buyer the impression that you have experience with this type of project—probably because you do have the experience, even if it's not with your current company or as an independent consultant.

If you haven't included this *been there, done that* information in your proposal before, you may be pleasantly surprised at how easy it is to design and develop this section.

- **Talk with people in your company.** Start by talking to the people in your company who actually implement your products. Your company's operational staff probably can give you everything you need for your proposal. But don't be surprised if they question your motives. Operational staff members always blame the sales guys for promising the world to customers, and now you're asking for their help. But you can win them over because they'll like the idea that they have some input into the implementation section, especially the schedule.

- **Share your knowledge about the buyer.** To give you some realistic estimates on the resources and time needed to complete the implementation, your operational staff probably needs to know something about the prospective buyer. They need to know things like background information about the buyer's business, how your proposed product can work in the buyer's company, and what benefits the buyer expects to receive—sections one and two of your proposal.

How we reassured a big buyer and won

In the late 1980s, I was a partner in a professional services firm that developed computer-based training programs to customer specifications. To put a price on a proposal, we had to work closely with the buyer to define the instructional objectives, curriculum design, and estimated course length by module or unit. We plugged all these estimates into a project planning system, and the system generated a price and a timeline for completion, which we put in our proposals. We also included the actual computer-generated report in an appendix to the proposal.

We closed a lot of business. Once we beat a big consulting group for a large project with one of the "Big Three" automobile manufacturers. One of the buyer's staff commented, "We know you guys are a small company, but you really seem to have a handle on how to do business."

He was referring to the implementation section in our winning proposal, and I guess he was saying, in effect, "We know you guys have been there and done that, so we think you can do it for us, too."

Titling the Implementation Section

Some generic section titles you can use for section three are listed below. Of course, you'll have to choose an appropriate title based on what you're selling.

- Implementation
- Product Installation
- Project Management
- Engagement Management
- Business Practices

Although a generic title works, consider customizing the section title. Because this section really discusses elements of your business, some logical titles can include your company's name:

- Union Data Systems: Conversion Management
- Security Technologies: Project Management Overview
- Mandrel & Jones: Engagement Practices

Optionally, you also can use the section title to focus the reader's attention on your proposed project:

- Custom Systems Development: ELS Security System
- Audit Services Transition and Engagement Practices for the New Wellstone Corporation
- Central Expressway Plaza Project: Construction Management

Deciding What Subsections to Include

To make a decision, a buyer needs to know how, with whom, and when you plan to implement your product. You address that need in the implementation section through the three standard subsections:

- Methods

- Team

- Schedule

You address what and how in the methods subsection, who in the team subsection, and when in the schedule subsection. Note that adding the seller's name or the product's name, and for some subsections the buyer's name, makes a proposal appear more customized.

As you develop the third section, keep in mind that your primary goal is to:

- Differentiate your company and its proposal from the competition.

- Assure the buyer that your company has implementation management capabilities and experience.

- Present your company's standard approach for doing business.

Deciding What to Include in the Implementation Management Subsection

Your proposal needs to assure the buyer that your company can manage the implementation team, resources, logistics, and activities for any size project, whether it takes less than a month to complete or lasts more than a year. The implementation management subsection should include the following information:

- Major project phases and activities within each phase

- Deliverables or end-products by phase

- Buyer review and approval points within each phase

Here are a few tips to help you design this section. These are tips on what not to do.

- Don't put too much detail into this section. Only include the major phases and important activities. Identify the significant deliverables or outputs that the buyer can review and approve.

- Don't worry about the project schedule for now. After you describe your major phases and activities, you can create a schedule that's easy to understand.

Keeping those details under control!

Several years ago, I developed a proposal model for a financial information software company. The company licenses software to small-to medium-sized financial institutions. Typically, its sales professionals sell to banks that either use a third-party data processing provider or have their own in-house system. If the buyer decides to license the new system, it has to go through a very complex software implementation and data conversion.

When I asked the professional services manager how they implement the system, he handed me a five-page list of 167 tasks—the company's installation checklist. It was thorough and quite impressive. But the five-page list was far too much for the proposal.

To solve the problem, we created six major implementation phases with five to ten major activities in each phase for the implementation section of the proposal. For each major phase, we also identified some deliverables that the buyer could review or approve. By organizing the details in this fashion, we created a useful part of a proposal.

The simple plan shown in Figure 7-2 illustrates a complex project plan for a software company.

Figure 7-2 Complex Project Plan

Phase	Activities	Deliverables
Project Planning	• Create preliminary Statement of Work (SOW) • Kickoff meeting to introduce project team	• Statement of Work (preliminary) • Project Team
Requirements Analysis	• Gather project requirements • Revise SOW • Customer approval of SOW • Start development of detailed Project Plan and System Design Specifications	• Revised and approved SOW

Phase	Activities	Deliverables
System Design	• Complete development of detailed Project Plan and System Design Specifications • Assign team resources • Customer approval of Project Plan and System Design Specifications	• Project Plan • System Design Specifications
System Development	• Develop system based on System Design Specifications • Unit test system as necessary • Test final system design for completeness and correctness	• Unit tested system
Implementation/ Installation	• Install Dialogue system onto customer's computers • End-to-end testing in customer environment • Signoff of installed and tested Dialogue	• Installed and tested system
System Testing	• Pre-production testing • Begin knowledge transfer of application to customer staff	• Production system
Project Closure	• Customer signoff for project • Customer completes Satisfaction Survey	• Ongoing operations

Writing About the Team

If your implementation methodology or project management subsection tells a buyer what your company does and how it does it, then the team subsection lets the buyer know who's going to do it. Most buyers like to see that a team is involved, especially when your proposed solution requires a complex or long implementation. Buyers also like the idea of a team if your company is providing ongoing service. A team subsection sends a strong message that your company knows what resources are needed to deliver on its obligations.

Including basic team information

In many situations, the team consists of people from the buyer's organization and yours. For example, a software company usually needs someone from the buyer's company to help it develop conversion program specifications to convert data from an old system to the new system. The software company may also need some buyer representatives to help it define processing options for the new system. Include the following information for each team member, whether the team member works for your organization or for the buyer:

- Organization name

- First and last name of the team member

- Corporate or functional title of the team member

Defining team roles and responsibilities

You can use the team subsection of your proposal to do two things:

- Clearly identify the critical team resources that are needed

- Make sure that the buyer understands its responsibilities in the implementation by including the roles and responsibilities of the buyer's team members

Writing a team subsection for every proposal may seem like a lot of work. But if your company uses a standard implementation management approach or follows standard business practices, team member roles and responsibilities don't change that much from one proposal to the next.

Including team member resumes in an appendix

Certified public accounting, consulting, and systems development firms, among others, may include biographical resumes of the people they plan to assign to the project. When a company is buying intangible services, their decision makers are probably interested in the education, experiences, and the past projects of the seller's staff. Think of this resume concept the next time you're sitting in the dentist chair reading the dentist's diploma hanging on the wall. You know the root canal will hurt, but at least you know that the dentist has learned the proper way to create the pain.

If your company sells professional services, consider including a biographical resume of each team member in an appendix.

Using a table to introduce a team

Figure 7-3 shows how you can use a chart to explain who does what on a complex team that includes both seller and buyer staff members. For this example, I'm calling the buyer *Wellstone Corporation* and the seller *ABC Software*. The seller's task is to implement a new document production system. Note the following features in the chart:

- Team members are grouped by buyer and seller organization.

- All team members have a specific role.

- The names and titles for all the team members are included.

- All team members have their primary responsibilities clearly defined

Figure 7-3 Team Subsection

Company	Position	Roles/Responsibilities
Wellstone Corporation	Project Sponsor	• Overall project responsibility • Issue resolution
	Project Manager	• Primary contact for ABC Software • Define project objectives • Coordinate WC resources • Develop and monitor project plan • Report to senior management
	Business Manager	• Provide knowledge of documents to be produced and related business rules of triggering paragraphs and data variables
	Database Administrator	• Provide knowledge of DBMS configuration and tuning
	Programmer	• Develop programs to format data to be included in documents • Advise from where data should be extracted
	Systems Administrator	• Provide knowledge of operating systems and utilities • Server configuration and tuning
ABC Software	Account Manager	• Primary contact for training, services, or additional modules. • Escalation point for project issues. • Responsible for overall customer satisfaction.
	Project Manager	• Define project objectives • Coordinate ABC Software resources • Develop and monitor project plan • Report to senior management
	Developer	• Develop custom programming • Convert and proof data
	Technician	• Provide knowledge of operating system, Web server, application server, and DBMS

Using a Schedule to Show When Things Get Done

Your proposal's implementation management subsection tells a buyer what you're going to do and how you're going to do it and your team subsection lets the buyer know who's going to do it. Finally, the schedule subsection gives the buyer information about when the implementation will happen. The information in this subsection is important to the buyer because it lets the buyer know when your proposed product will be installed and it will start realizing the benefits.

Your schedule subsection assures the buyer that you've thought about everything that's needed to complete its implementation. This subsection can include the major phases or activities and realistic dates for completing the project. You can use high-level bar charts or tables that reference an appendix for more detail. Remember that your schedule subsection must coordinate with the project phases and activities that you define in your implementation management subsection.

You can present a schedule very simply in a table showing the phases and their start and stop dates, as shown in Figure 7-4. Or, you could use a bar chart to show the project schedule.

Figure 7-4 Simple Project Schedule

Phase	Start	Stop
Project Planning	03/26/07	04/09/07
Requirements Analysis	04/12/07	04/23/07
System Design	04/24/07	06/05/07
System Development	05/10/07	06/30/07
Implementation/ Installation	07/05/07	07/15/07
System Testing	07/18/07	07/31/07
Project Closure	08/05/07	08/10/07
Ongoing Support	08/11/07	

Figure 7-4 probably provides enough detail for decision makers. It sends a strong message that the seller has really thought about the project.

Using a Table to Show Team Commitment

You can include an optional table in your implementation section that shows team commitment by project phase. This table has one purpose: to show team member commitment levels for each phase of the implementation or project. A table like this also lets the buyer know how much of their team members' time you expect on the project. For smaller projects, identifying the buyer's team commitment levels may not be that big of an issue. But for long or complex projects where the seller needs expertise and cooperation from the buyer's organization, it makes a lot of sense to include this type of table in the implementation section of your proposal.

Figure 7-5 shows a team commitment by project phase table. It combines information from two subsections and it:

- Uses the project phases from the implementation subsection

- Includes the organization, team member, and team member role information from the team subsection

Figure 7-5 Team Commitment by Project Phase Table

Organization	Name	Project Role	% Time Commitment by Phase					
			1	2	3	4	5	6
FNB	Ann Gollen	Conversion Liaison	50	25	25	50	50	25
	Gene Sills	Application Specialist	35	10	25	40	50	10
	Jack Denton	Application Specialist	35	10	25	40	50	10
	Julie Anderson	Customer Service Rep.	35	10	25	40	50	10
FSCS	John Fischer	Conversion Team Leader	50	50	50	50	50	20
	Angela Carter	Bank Liaison Rep.	40	20	40	75	90	20
	Ted Krause	Conversion Specialist	90	90	90	50	50	0
	Bill Gander	Customer Service Rep.	50	50	25	75	90	10
	Randy Lealand	Installation Specialist	50	25	25	75	25	10

Figure 7-6 Sections 1–3 of the Five Section Proposal Structure

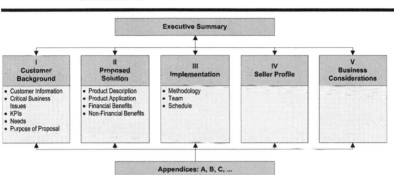

Stuff to Remember

Johnny and his team probably learned more about how the company implements its products than they wanted. The director of professional services took them step by step through their project scoping and scheduling process. At the end of her presentation, she did give them a one-page methodology table that defines the company's implementation phases, activities, and deliverables—perfect for the proposal. She also developed the Project Team subsection for them. She thought it would help the buyer understand what resources they would need to commit to an implementation. Everyone agreed that sales and professional services would collaborate on setting implementation dates in their proposals.

√ One of the functions of the third section, implementation, is to reassure the buyer that you can deliver on the contract. This section can send the buyer a strong *been there, done that* message.

√ To help make a buy decision, the buyer needs to know how, with whom, and when you plan to implement your product. Use three standard subsections: methodology, team, and schedule.

8

Section 4: Focusing on the Seller (It's about Time!)

Johnny and his team agreed that they had developed the most difficult parts of their new proposal model—the sections that defined the buyer's issues and needs, presented their solution and value proposition, and defined how their company implemented the product. Johnny had to admit the professional services director had been very helpful. She virtually wrote the "Implementation" section for them and was very happy to do it. She even suggested how her group would work with sales to develop the custom proposals by estimating resource requirements and critical project dates.

Now the team was debating what a decision maker would want to read next. Some thought it was time to present the business considerations such as pricing and terms and conditions. Scott, the sales professional who had lost the big deal, reminded everyone that they really had developed a solid business case for selecting their company's product, but had not really said anything about the company itself.

Johnny agreed and suggested they should start by asking their customers what they wanted to know about the company before they had made their buy decisions. Johnny directed the team members to talk with four to five of their best customers. Ask them some questions about why they selected the company. Better yet, ask them if they had developed vendor selection criteria.

The way I design sales proposals, the section describing you the seller, which features you or your company, does not come at the beginning (like some people like to write their proposals). It doesn't even rate second billing. I hold back this part for late in the proposal. It's not until the fourth main section that you tell the buyer all about you or your company, which may create a dilemma for egocentric sellers. Figure 8-1 shows you the overall view of the proposal, with the subsections for section one through four filled in.

Figure 8-1 Sections 1–4 of the Five Section Proposal Structure

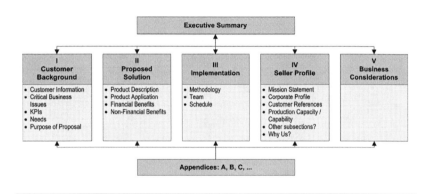

Sales and Proposal Development: Process Integration for Section Four

Like section three, the fourth section doesn't contain as much *process connections information* (PCI) as the first two sections. And, as you might guess, there aren't as many *common activities* in your sales proposal development process needed to develop it. Note that you might want to review Chapter 2 and Figure 2-1, which introduce these terms.

You can develop parts of this section without knowing anything about the buyer—this represents the standard information that you want to include in every proposal. However, don't treat this fourth section like it's boilerplate. Besides, I never use the term boilerplate—the *politically correct* term is "standard wording." There is one subsection in this section that absolutely requires buyer knowledge to complete it—*Why*

Us? Figure 8-2 uses a variation of Figure 3-1 to highlight those sales tools, which are sources of PCI for section four.

Figure 8-2 Sources of PCI Used in Section 4

Sales Tools	Process Connections Information									
	Background Information	Critical Business Issues, KPIs	Impacts on Business	Customer Stated Needs	Customer's Selection Criteria	Product/Service Application	Prices/Fees	Non-Financial Benefits	Financial Benefits	Implementation/ Installation Variables
Customer Intelligence	S	S								
Customer's Web Site	S	S								
Prospect Survey	S	S		S	**S**					
Buyer Questionnaire	S	S	S	S	**S**					
KPI Input (Key Pain Indicator)	U	S		S						
Pricing/Configure System		U		U		S	S			S
ROI Valuation	U	S	S	S		U	U		S	
Sales Process Letters (various	U	U	U	U	U	U	U	S	U	U
Sales Proposal	U	U	U	U	**U**	U	U	U	U	U

The logic for waiting until late in the proposal to introduce your company is as follows:

- First, the buyer wants to know that you know something about its unique business operations, that you have identified some critical business issue or issues, and that you understand its needs.

- Next, the buyer wants to see if your product can really make a difference for its company. Can it help the company resolve the critical business issues, and does it offer the company some financial and non-financial benefits?

- Then, if the buyer thinks you understand its situation and likes your proposed product, your proposal needs to convince the buyer that you're able to implement the product.

  After reading all this in your proposal—and being impressed—the buyer asks, "Hey, who are these guys?"

Understanding the Purposes for Section Four

As you can see in Figure 8-1, the part where you talk about yourself is the fourth main section of the proposal structure that I recommend. The fourth section's purpose is to:

- Reduce the buyer's risk in making a change or doing business with your company

- Give the buyer information about your company's qualifications and capabilities

- Tell the buyer how your company is very qualified to help it achieve its improvement opportunity

In some ways, section three, implementation (see Chapter 7), and this fourth section—all about you—have similar purposes: they both help reduce the buyer's risk. Both parts assure the buyer that you have the experience, capabilities, and resources to deliver on the contract. Remember that if your proposed solution represents a critical purchase, then the decision makers feel these two types of risk:

- **Business risk:** A wrong decision may adversely affect their company.

- **Personal risk:** They'll look bad or get blamed if they make a poor or wrong decision.

Getting Off the Level Playing Field

Many buyers develop selection criteria to evaluate vendors in complex sales situations. Buyers quickly drop those sellers who don't meet the criteria. The remaining sellers make the buyer's shortlist. Consciously or unconsciously, the buyer may put all shortlist sellers on a level playing field. In other words, the buyer might think that all the shortlist sellers are equally qualified, so it doesn't spend additional time studying the sellers' qualifications.

You can't stop the buyer from using selection criteria to decide which vendors are on the short list. But you can use section four of your sales proposal to rise above the crowd. A well-crafted seller profile can really help you differentiate your company, highlight your employees, and explain the way you do business. Further, your well-crafted seller profile section just may force the buyer into reevaluating its shortlist contenders—some of your competitors may not like that.

Selling the Buyer on Your Company

Your seller profile section gives the buyer reasons why it should buy your products and do business with you instead of one of your competitors. This section gives a newer company a chance to really convince a buyer that, while it may be new, it really has its act together. And a long client list may not impress the buyer as much as an innovative process or a new approach to service delivery.

Don't use this section just to impress the buyer with how big your company is or how many employees and locations it has. Being big doesn't instantly qualify your company as the best choice for the buyer. Instead, use this section to impress the buyer with your company's unique qualifications.

Different subsections for different buyers

You may want to insert special subsections for specific buyers. For example, if a buyer is concerned with your company's disaster recovery plans, include a subsection on disaster recovery. You may end up developing lots of special subsections that you can select depending on the buyer (this is pretty easy if you're using an automated proposal production system). I give you more information on optional subsections later in the chapter. Just remember you need to use this section to sell a buyer on your company. Each buyer is unique and has unique information needs and selection criteria. A sales professional just needs to learn which hot buttons that he has to push.

Answering the buyer's questions

Let's go back to the concept that your proposal gives you an opportunity to have a private conversation with the decision makers. So, design this main section like you're being quizzed by one of the buyer's decision makers. The decision maker is playing the old twenty questions game with you to find out what he wants to know about your company. Remember that each buyer has its list of twenty questions. Some of the questions are very similar, but others are unique. Part of your consultative sales and proposal development processes is finding out what the buyer wants to know about your company.

As you decide how to develop your seller profile section for each buyer, think about these questions:

- What kinds of questions has the buyer asked about my company?

- What are the buyer's top three to five selection criteria?

- What really seem to be important issues or concerns in the buyer's company?

Titling Section Four

Since this section profiles you the seller, including your name in the title makes sense. Here are some examples:

- ROI4Sales Profile

- Corporate Overview: Electronic Learning Systems

- Royce, Jones, and Smith: Business Profile

Deciding What Subsections to Use

The seller profile section is different from the other proposal sections. It doesn't have a list of recommended subsections like the other four sections. Rather, the seller profile section has suggested subsections that you should consider using. However, you should always consider using the following subsections in your seller profile section because they say a lot about your company:

- Mission or Business Philosophy Statement

- Company Overview

- Customer References
- Why Us?

Consider your buyer's information needs and its risks to help you decide what other subsections you may want to include in your seller profile section. Your conversations with the buyer can help you identify what information the buyer may want to see in this section. The seller's business type or profession also helps determine which subsections to include in the seller profile section of a proposal.

The following pages contain detailed information and examples for the four recommended subsections for the seller profile section.

Mission statement subsection

Putting your mission statement or business philosophy in your proposal represents one of the best ways to assure the buyer that you or your company can deliver on the contract. The content of the mission statement gives the buyer a good idea of what the company is all about. Most company mission statements are brief—one paragraph. Your mission statement can set the tone for the rest of your seller profile subsection; therefore, you may want to start your fourth section with your mission statement.

Company overview subsection

Use this subsection to give your buyer some insight and background on your company. You can use it to publicize your company's annual revenues, number of employees, number of locations, and so on. However, always try to keep this subsection (and the entire section four) as buyer-specific as possible.

Depending on the buyer's needs or selection criteria, you can find it beneficial to customize this apparently static subsection. For example, a buyer may only want to work with a small firm. To help satisfy this selection criterion, one of our clients, a large international firm, uses its company overview subsection to emphasize its local office philosophy and the continuity of its office managers.

When designing this subsection, you might get some help from two internal sources, your:

- Marketing department
- Company's Web site

Remember that the marketing department is responsible for customer communications. Tell it what you're doing and ask it to write a short (two- to three-paragraph) company overview to use in the company's sales proposals. Marketing can be very helpful. If the marketing guys are helpful, talk to them about writing different company overview subsections:

- For each of the company's target markets
- To address different buyer selection criteria

If your company has a Web site, you can start developing this subsection by copying information directly from the "About Us" page on your site.

These two company overview examples can give you some ideas how different types of companies may write this subsection. The first example is from one of our client's proposals with the names changed to protect the innocent and the numbers inflated to impress this book's readers. I developed the other examples by using information from Web sites. See, it's pretty easy.

Sales vs. Marketing

While working with a client that sells digital archiving solutions, I suggested to the VP of sales that he ask marketing for some ideas and content for the seller profile section of the new proposal models. I stated, "Marketing is responsible for customer communications and we want to include the best, most accurate, and 'factory-approved' wording in our new proposals." The VP of Marketing was surprised at the request but very elated (perhaps he had seen some of the old proposals that were sent to prospective customers). He assigned one of his staff to our proposal design project. Our proposal models contain some very well-crafted seller information including variable content based on a buyer's vertical market.

The following company overview subsection example uses a chronological history of the company to show buyers the company's important achievements and milestones.

Corporate Overview: FTI Overview

Financial Technologies, Inc. (FTI) is one of the fastest growing financial service software companies in the United States. Revenues last year exceeded $125 million. Its corporate headquarters are in Scottsdale, Arizona; however, the company has sales and customer support staff in its Chicago and Philadelphia offices. Over 300 financial service, customer support, and data processing professionals work for FTI.

Corporate History

7/02   Financial Technologies, Inc. (FTI) founded.

1/03   IBM announces FTI as a National Business Partner.

2/04   FTI introduces the BankSystem 2000 family of software at the American Bankers Association Annual Conference.

5/04   FTI successfully installs the first *BankSystem 2000* beta site.

3/05   FTI introduces the BankSystem Plus 2000 product line to the banking industry.

7/05   FTI acquires Pegasus, Inc., a Denver-based platform automation company with over 200 clients.

6/06   FTI acquires iBank, Inc., a Milwaukee-based Internet banking software company with 55 worldwide clients.

7/07   FTI installs BankSystem Plus 2000 at the 40th customer site.

The following company overview subsection is one for a manufacturing company. I used a company's Web site to get information and have changed names and some of the content.

Company Overview: Daniels Engineering & Manufacturing Company

A leader in manufacturing solutions

Daniels Engineering & Manufacturing Company is a leader in providing manufacturing solutions for North and Latin American companies. Daniels has three plants in Dallas, Texas. The company has a 32-year heritage of providing reliable, innovative manufacturing solutions for aerospace markets.

Daniels develops customized manufacturing solutions for its customers by integrating modular control components. These components can be used to develop solutions that range from manual to fully-automated manufacturing processes.

Daniels's breadth of product and application capabilities has enabled the company to develop a number of revolutionary manufacturing solutions that have become aerospace industry standards over the last two decades. Daniels also has complete research and development, design engineering, manufacturing, project management, and installation service capabilities to assure it customers that its manufacturing solutions are developed to specifications and delivered on time.

Customer reference subsection

Prospective decision makers like to see customer references. They do two things:

- Let the buyer know that they're not the first to buy from the seller

- Make it easy for the buyer to talk to someone who has experience with the seller's company

The buyer may never check your references. What matters is the fact that you're confident enough to include references in your proposal. Customer references say a lot about your company. While reading your customer references, a decision maker may think, "ABC Company is one of their references; we know how tough those guys are!"

Make it easy for a buyer to check your customer references. Include the following information for each reference:

- Company name
- Company address (city, state, and zip code)
- Contact name and title
- Contact telephone number and, optionally, e-mail address

You might want to include other information to help the buyer decide if it wants to check a reference such as: date implemented, installed, or customer-since date and type of product installed, or other information that can show a reference's size or other characteristics.

Before you include a customer reference in you sales proposal, make sure that doing so is okay with the customer.

Customer list versus customer references

A customer list is just that: a list of customers. No contact information is provided. Some sellers like to include a customer list in their proposals, especially if their customer list is long and impressive. Some of our clients like to list customers within a market segment. Their sales professionals select which market segments to include in their proposals (of course, this is easy to do if you have an automated proposal production system).

Remember that you're not making it very easy for the buyer to talk to someone at a company that's included on your customer list. If you decide to include customer references and a customer list, think about putting your customer references in a subsection of section four and putting your customer list in an appendix.

The very important *Why Us?* subsection

Always make the *Why Us?* subsection the last subsection in the seller profile section. This subsection is intended to pull everything together for the reader. The *Why Us?* subsection actually finishes the real creative part of your proposal because the next and last section of the sales proposal only deals with business stuff (pricing details, payment schedule, terms and conditions, warranties, etc).

The *Why Us?* subsection is different from all the other subsections in your sales proposal. You use it to actually tell the buyer why your company is the best choice. Many sellers never think about including a

Why Us? subsection in their proposals. Maybe they're not sufficiently egocentric.

A Why Us? subsection helps you link critical components of your sales and proposal processes. A well-written *Why Us?* subsection can help make some very clear connections for the buyer's decision makers. It can connect:

- The buyer's critical business issues with your proposed solution

- Your proposed product's features and benefits with the buyer's needs

- Your capacity to deliver on the contract and your company's capabilities, operations, and characteristics with the buyer's key selection criteria

Many sellers assume that by the time a decision maker has read this far in the sales proposal, these connections should be obvious. But you know what happens when we make assumptions...

Read this subsection. Do you think it links the critical components of the sale and proposal?

Why ElectroBill?

ElectroBill's EBPP system is the best option because it lets the City of Westerville:

1. Select and integrate a multiple billing type application for its current and future EBPP needs

2. Use off-the-shelf, low-cost hardware to host its EBPP application

3. Reach high levels of customer acceptance through its *direct* EBPP model

4. Through its proven implementation approach, ElectroBill can ensure a smooth implementation to an operational EBPP system.

Selecting Optional Subsections

You need to consider some optional subsections for your seller profile section. As you design this section, think about how you can make it more buyer specific. Try to put yourself in the buyer's position. What would you want to know about a seller's business if it were your decision?

Table 8-1 lists some optional seller profile subsections to consider:

Table 8-1 Optional Seller Subsections

Optional Subsection	Description / Comments / Use
Research and Development	Technology is changing so rapidly that most people can't keep up with it. Depending upon your customers and your business or profession, keeping up with technology may be very important. If your company sells networking hardware and software or builds automated machinery maintenance systems, then the buyer probably wants to know about your company's R&D program. Your buyers probably want to know how much you spend each year on R&D and what part your R&D budget is of your company's total budget.
Staff	A subsection on staff can be an important part of your proposal, especially if your company is a professional service or consulting firm. In these situations, the education, experience, and competency of the company's staff usually has some relationship to the quality of the service the firm provides. Use this subsection to write about the people who deliver service for your company. Include your staff's years of experience and education, your company's certification requirements for consultants or professionals, and your company's ongoing staff training programs. Remember that this subsection usually ties to the team subsection in section three. If you have several staff members working on the project, consider putting this information in an appendix.

Optional Subsection	*Description / Comments / Use*
Facilities and Equipment	Having a facilities and equipment subsection in your proposal may be important, depending on what you sell. If your company sells data processing services, it's a more important subsection than if your company provides consulting services.
Quality	Back in the 1980s, people became more aware of quality than ever before and demanded quality in the goods and services they purchased and how they were treated as customers. Many companies implemented Total Quality Management and ISO/9000 programs to achieve world-class quality levels. Now most buyers just expect that whatever they buy will be top quality.

It may seem that all the media hype surrounding the "quality movement" has decreased, but you still should show in your sales proposal how you can satisfy your buyer's demand for quality. |
| **Production Capacities** | Besides wanting to know what facilities and equipment your company uses, the buyer may want to know how quickly you can deliver. For example, if your company manufactures custom commercial-grade windows and is submitting a proposal to do all the windows for a new 400-room hotel, the architect and building contractor probably are very interested in how long it will take your company to build the windows. |
| **Customer Service** | This is a hot button in an economy that is very service oriented. Many buyers want to know how your company provides customer service. Your proposal needs to give them some information about your company's customer service philosophy, people, training, facilities, hours, systems, and procedures. |

Optional Subsection	Description / Comments / Use
Systems Design and Development	If you sell software application systems, buyers may want to know how your company designs and develops its systems, especially if the buyer plans to use your systems to run a critical operation in its company.

Stuff to Remember

Johnny watched in amazement as his team quickly agreed what to include in the seller profile section. Each one had spent time asking their best customers what they wanted to know about an unknown seller's company. Rather than creating a lengthy section filled with lots of hype, the team needed only two pages to describe the important things about company. They did spend some time working on the guidelines for the "Why Us" subsection including the development of several real-life examples. Everyone agreed; this had been the easiest section to write.

√ You can develop parts of this section without knowing anything about the buyer—this represents the standard information that you want to include in every proposal. However, don't treat this fourth section like it's boilerplate.

√ There is one subsection in this section that absolutely requires buyer knowledge to complete it—*Why us?*

√ The seller profile section has four suggested subsections that you should consider using:

- Mission or Business Philosophy
- Company Overview
- Customer References
- Why Us?

√ Consider some optional subsections for your seller profile section to make it more buyer-specific. Put yourself in the buyer's position. What would you want to know about a seller's business if it were your decision? (See Table 8-1 for a list of some optional subsections to consider.)

9

Section 5: Defining the Business Considerations Stuff

Finally! Johnny and his team agreed they only have one main section left to design—the section that will contain all the business stuff that they haven't yet covered in the first four sections. One of the team made an interesting observation, "We have the total price in our 'Financial Benefits' subsection, but none of the details. So all we need in this section are the details and we're done!"

Johnny initially agreed but suggested that before they all headed for the golf course, they should list anything they could think of related to pricing, invoicing, or other business considerations of their deals. He was particularly interested in any problems they had experienced in the past including when they worked for other companies. Johnny stated the team had done an exceptional job designing the first four sections of their new proposal model. He didn't want to finish with a sub-standard section.

This chapter is about the boring business stuff you have to put into your sales proposals—the standard provisions about assumptions, fees, and schedules. In our five-part proposal plan (see Figure 9-1), we lump all of these items together as *business considerations*. Writing about business considerations may bore you and your buyer may get bored reading this section. But believe me, the business considerations section of your proposal is a very important part of the deal.

This section answers basic questions the buyer's decision makers have when they evaluate your proposals. Remember, view your proposal as the private conversation you are having with the decision makers. During the conversation, they may ask you these questions:

- What assumptions did you make about the timing and pricing of the project?

- What is the total fee or price to install the proposed product or implement the proposed service?

- What additional charges should we expect?

- What terms and conditions will you require for the deal?

- When will you bill us and for how much?

One of the ways to think about the purpose of this section is that it gets you and the buyer on the same page. You may be that lucky sales professional who's never had a misunderstanding about price or some other expenses. In a past company, I wasn't so lucky!

Here's a good example. Suppose that *you* thought the buyer understood that travel expenses were extra but the *buyer* thought they were part of your price—a crash and burn about to happen. Think of the implications for this looming discussion. If the buyer refuses to pay your travel expenses, your profits drop. If you convince the buyer it has to pay your travel expenses, you may have a very unhappy customer with diminished opportunities for future business.

You might think of this last main proposal section as an informal contract. Use it to cover business considerations that you didn't present in a previous proposal section, but that are critical to your company's ability to maintain its profitability. But don't make this section read like a legal document. Just write it to avoid surprises for everyone after the sale.

Sales and Proposal Development: Process Integration for Section Five

Like sections three and four, this fifth and last section doesn't contain as much *process connections information* (PCI) as the first two sections. You'll also find that there aren't as many *common activities* in your sales proposal development process needed to develop it.

Some parts of this section can be developed without knowing anything about the buyer. These parts represent the standard information that you want to include in every proposal, such as your pricing components or your invoicing policy. But don't treat this fifth section like boilerplate. Every buyer is unique and so are the business considerations surrounding the proposed deal. Figure 9-1 uses a variation of Figure 3-1 to highlight those sales tools, which are sources of PCI for section five.

Figure 9-1 Sources of PCI Used in Section 4

Sales Tools	Process Connections Information									
	Background Information	Critical Business Issues, KPI's	Impacts on Business	Customer Stated Needs	Customer's Selection Criteria	Product/Service Application	Prices/Fees	Non-Financial Benefits	Financial Benefits	Implementation/ Installation Variables
Customer Intelligence	S	S								
Customer's Web Site	S	S								
Prospect Survey	S	S		S	S					
Buyer Questionnaire	S	S	S	S	S					
KPI Input (Key Pain Indicator)	U	S		S						
Pricing/Configure System		U		U		S	S			S
ROI Valuation	U	S	S	S		U	U		S	
Sales Process Letters (various)	U	U	U	U	U	U	U	S	U	U
Sales Proposal	U	U	U	U	U	**U**	**U**	U	U	**U**

Titling Section Five

Since this section deals with money and other business stuff, you can reference content in the section's title. Here are some examples:

- Business Considerations
- Costs and Commitments
- Project Investment
- Fees and Expenses

Deciding What Subsections to Include

Three subsections are very common in the business considerations section of a sales proposal. You will probably include them in every one of your proposals:

- Assumptions
- Fees/Prices and other expenses
- Invoicing schedule

Optional subsections

Depending on the type of business or profession that your company is in, you may want or need to include one or more of these optional subsections:

- Terms and conditions
- Warranty and/or guarantee statements
- Environmental policies
- General service conditions (regarding how services will be performed, often used by professional services firms)
- Non-disclosure statement
- Regulatory statements, such as a statement defining the seller's compliance with equal employment opportunity regulations

Often, your legal department takes care of the wording for these optional subsections. Some lawyers just need to be productive when they're not chasing ambulances (just kidding; I don't want to get a subpoena or restraining order).

Writing About Assumptions

As a seller, you might make assumptions about certain aspects of the buyer's business to help establish your fees or prices, assign your resources, and schedule your installation, implementation, or engagement. You can usually base your assumptions on:

* Applicable aspects of the buyer's business and operations

* Experiences you've had with similar engagements, projects, implementations, or production situations

* Your estimates of the scope and magnitude of the proposed solution for the buyer's unique situation

* Internal or external estimates of business and economic trends that may affect the buyer's business or your business

For example, one of our clients sells fractional ownership of corporate aircraft. It has an adjustment in flight costs that is tied to jet fuel prices.

Always keep the buyer in mind while writing this subsection. Your assumptions subsection should answer any remaining questions that the buyer's decision makers have about your proposed product after they've read the first four sections of the proposal.

Two rules to follow when developing assumptions for your sales proposals are:

* Include only critical assumptions, and not more than four or five.

* If you have too many assumptions, look at section two of your proposal (the proposed solution) or section three (the implementation) and ask yourself whether the assumptions you've saved for the end of the proposal really should be dealt with in these earlier sections. More about this later.

Identifying critical assumptions

As you write your proposal, especially the parts that deal with the price and your implementation schedule, follow these steps to identify your critical assumptions:

1. Think about how you develop the price and schedule the implementation for the buyer.

   Are you basing the price and schedule on everything going according to plan? How often does that happen?

2. Think about what could happen to make the project cost more and reduce your profits.

   At this point, your experience in the business can make a difference. Think about past deals that were similar. Did you have a problem with any them? If so, what caused things to go wrong? If you're new to your company, ask a coworker for help. If everybody is new to the company (or if the company is new), hold a brainstorming session to figure out what could go wrong after the sale.

3. Take the answers that you get when you ask yourself or a coworker what could go wrong or the ideas from the brainstorming session. Your assumptions are that none of these things will happen.

Here are some more examples of assumptions. I've included one that I personally experienced:

- To develop its implementation schedule, a software development firm assumed that the buyer would review and approve systems design documents within five business days of receipt.

- To maintain the equipment prices listed in the proposal over the term of the proposed agreement, a manufacturer assumed that its raw material costs would not increase by more than 5 percent during the scheduled production run.

- What would happen to the manufacturer's profitability if the cost of one of the key production materials jumped 15 percent during the agreement?

- When developing an audit fee quote, a CPA firm assumed that the client would provide workspace and administrative support for the firm's auditors during the audit.

- What would happen if the client didn't give the auditors workspace and administrative support? Doing the audit would be a lot more difficult for the CPA firm. The audit would take more time to complete, and time is money.

- *Here's my real-life example.* I was a partner in a professional services firm that developed custom computer-based training (CBT) courseware. We always included one assumption in our proposals that stated the client's staff would review and approve our design documents in five business days. Normally, we had few problems with our clients meeting these review deadlines.

However, the subject matter experts for one large client were a bit overworked and some had attitudes. They didn't place much priority on reviewing and approving our design documents. Day by day, the project schedule slipped. This slippage caused the productivity of our instructional designers and CBT authors to drop. More important, it lowered our productivity on the entire project—we weren't loosing money but our margins were in the tank.

I asked the project manager to determine how much time and money the client's delays had cost us. Over a three-month period, the delays had cost $70,000. I met with the client's vice president and our project manager. We laid out our case and referenced our project plan and proposal; both clearly identified the five-day review period as scheduling assumptions. He agreed to pay an additional $70,000 for the project.

If you were writing any of the proposal types in the above list, would you include these assumptions in the business issues section? Think about the consequences if you didn't and something went wrong after the sale. Who would get the biggest surprise and be most adversely affected if these assumptions weren't included in your proposals and something went wrong?

Caution: Avoiding too many assumptions

Having too many assumptions in your proposal can be as bad as not having any—the buyer may not take any of them very seriously. As a rule, you probably don't want more than four or five assumptions in your assumptions subsection.

Having too many assumptions in your proposal may point to content problems elsewhere in your proposal. Take a hard look at the content and level of detail in sections two and three: the proposed solution and the implementation. You may be using the assumptions subsection to make up for deficiencies in these sections.

- **Section two: description and application subsections.** Rather than clearly describing your product and then defining its application in the buyer's business in section two, you may be using the assumption subsection to define specifications. Or, you may be making assumptions to explain how your product will be installed. You can correct these problems by moving some assumptions to section two and including these assumptions in your product description or application definition.

- **Section three: implementation.** You may be using assumptions instead of defining team members' roles and responsibilities, project or engagement activities and deliverables, or the schedule. By writing a better section three, you can cut down on the number of assumptions in your assumptions subsection.

Defining Fees or Prices

If the proposal you design follows our structure and content recommendations, the buyer's decision makers will have seen your fees or prices two times before they get to the price subsection of your proposal—first in the executive summary and then in the financial benefits subsection of section two.

The prices listed in the executive summary and financial benefits subsection are typically summary totals. Your proposal should present financial details and explanations in the price subsection of the business considerations section. You use this subsection to disclose and detail the buyer's total costs.

Remember that the goal of section five is to avoid buyer and seller surprises down the road. The more detail you include in the price subsection, the fewer surprises the buyer and you will have after the sale.

Some price subsection variations

Different sellers put different price information in their proposals. Your price subsection's content can vary because of several factors, including:

- Your company's business type and accepted pricing practices
- The buyer's information needs and expectations
- The need to:
  - Disclose fees or prices by project phase to support periodic invoices
  - Disclose project-related expenses, such as freight, travel costs, duplication, and so on
  - Show quantity, description, unit price, and extended price for products or product components

For example:

- A manufacturing company might list quantities, descriptions, unit prices, and extended prices for its product components. Additionally, its proposal may include applicable taxes and freight.

- A professional services firm might list fees by project phase with a grand total for the project. It also would include estimated travel expenses, if any.

Including all other expenses

Follow these two rules when deciding which expenses to include in your proposal:

- Rule 1: Include all possible expenses in your proposal.

- Rule 2: See Rule 1.

Remember, you want to avoid buyer and seller surprises after the sale. Make sure that your price subsection includes everything that you expect the buyer to pay for as part of the deal. This can include such things as:

- Freight, shipping, and handling

- Travel expenses

- Copying, printing, and postage

- Sales and other taxes

- Site preparation

- License fees (for required applications or operating systems)

- Equipment rental or lease payments (other than what you're selling or including in the deal)

One of our clients with thirty offices and more than sixty-five sales professionals uses Sales Document Builder, our automated proposal production system. Interestingly, client offices in different parts of the country wanted to list prices and fees differently. Some offices in the South combined "Materials and Labor" while offices in the Midwest said their clients always wanted these items listed as separate line items. We solved the problem by designing proposals with all the possible pricing components—fourteen pricing line items. The client's sales professionals simply picked from the list of pricing options when they were developing a proposal. When our system generated the proposals, it listed the exact pricing variables needed for the client's customer and as traditionally priced from the sales professional's office.

Here's an example of a price subsection.

Investment Detail

Maximum Security Systems will complete the project as outlined in the Implementation section. Any material or service that changes the scope of work may require an adjustment to the project fee.

Investment Breakdown:

Project Installation and Engineering Labor	$ 6,500
Materials and Equipment	11,000
System Maintenance (1st year)	2,200
Sub-Contractor Labor	1,500
Shipping	750
Taxes	660
Project Investment	**$22,610**

Explaining the invoicing schedule

Your proposal should let the buyer know how and when you will invoice. Use the invoicing schedule subsection to clearly explain how you calculate the amount of your invoices and when you plan to send them. Further, your proposal's invoicing schedule subsection can become very important if you link the timing of an invoice to the completion of a major project phase or deliverable.

For example, one of our clients, a company that sells turnkey computer systems, sends invoices to a buyer for:

- Fifty percent of the hardware costs when the buyer signs the contract and percentages of total software costs at the end of each project phase

- The remainder of hardware costs upon completion of installation or acceptance testing

- Travel expenses for the company's implementation team members at the end of each month

Figure 9-2 Sections 1–5 of the Five Section Proposal Structure

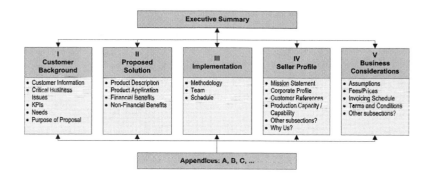

Stuff to Remember

Everyone on the team agreed that their proposal's "Investment" section was the easiest to develop of all the five sections. The toughest part was deciding if they needed an "Assumptions" subsection and then developing a few pricing and scheduling assumptions. They decided this section would contain several major investment variables and a grand total. They also decided to use an appendix to list the detailed pricing of the proposed system's components and to use that total from the appendix as the "System" line item in this proposal section. Johnny planned to ask Dave, his boss, if he should get legal to review it.

√ Section five contains the boring business stuff you have to put into your sales proposals—the standard provisions about assumptions, fees, and schedules.

√ Depending on the type of business or profession that your company is in, you may want or need to include one or more of these optional subsections such as: environmental policies or regulatory compliance statements.

√ As a seller, you need an 'Assumptions' subsection. You may make assumptions to establish your fees or prices, assign your resources, and schedule your installation, implementation, or engagement.

√ The goal of section five is to avoid buyer and seller surprises. The more detail you include, the fewer surprises the buyer and you will have after the sale.

10

Writing an Executive Summary and Transmittal Letter

Johnny and his team were admiring their new proposal model when Rich, said, "Hey, we're not done! What about a cover page and table of contents? And what about those appendices we said were needed to support some of the subsections? Scott jumped in and added, "At my last company we had to write an executive summary for every proposal plus a cover letter."

Johnny agreed and commented that they were never going to make it to the golf course. Of course, Rich and Scott were right. There were a few finishing touches left. If they were going to design their industry's benchmark proposal, they needed to finish strong. After a brief discussion, the team agreed that their new proposal model was missing five things:

- *Transmittal letter*
- *Executive Summary*
- *Title Page*
- *Table of Contents*
- *Appendices*

Johnny assigned each of his sales professionals to investigate one of the five remaining components and make recommendations. They would meet next week to finish the project. As a parting comment, Johnny also asked the team to start thinking about how they were going to package their new proposal.

This chapter and the next discuss these five components and packaging. If you really want to have a top-notch proposal, you will find some helpful guidelines, tips, and examples in these two chapters.

Decision makers live in a busy world, and reading your proposal just puts another demand on their schedules. Even though you might have developed the best proposal ever, some decision makers don't have the time to read every sentence. Actually, most people don't read anymore, they skim or scan. They only read the portions that interest them. One thing is for sure: they won't miss your price section!

If you did a good job designing, writing, and producing your sales proposal, even the skimmers and scanners will notice. They may sense that your proposal is top notch even if they don't read it carefully. However, you can count on most decision makers to take the time to read your proposal. They're aware of its importance to their company and they want to take the time to make a good decision. You can help them use that time effectively by adding two important components: the transmittal letter and executive summary. This chapter shows you how to produce these small but crucial components.

Understanding the Purposes

The transmittal letter represents your proposal's cover letter. And the executive summary, just as its name implies, is a summary of the proposal. If you design these two components correctly, both can frame your proposal by alerting readers to what's important—what you really want them to read and understand. They can work together as follows:

- **A transmittal letter** can focus your proposal's readers because it:

  - Gives your reasons for presenting the proposal to the buyer

  - Highlights the buyer's critical issues and your proposed solution

- **An executive summary** also can focus your proposal's readers because it captures the essence of your proposal by:

  - Providing summary information on all the key points contained within the proposal

  - Alerting readers to the critical information contained in the proposal's main sections

Some decision makers might only read your transmittal letter and the proposal's executive summary. They know from experience that these two proposal components, if well written, can provide them a heads up of your entire proposal and valuable insight into the sales situation. They may rely entirely on these two proposal components to prepare for your presentation if you get to make one. In these situations, your transmittal letter and executive summary play a critical role in positioning the reader for the sale.

In other instances, the heads up provided by your transmittal letter and executive summary may convince a few readers that their critical business issues and your proposed solution make some sense and need further study. If some decision makers briefly skim your proposal and only read the transmittal letter and executive summary, they might realize that they should either read your entire proposal or pass it down to a subordinate to review and report back.

Writing an Executive Summary

Your proposal's executive summary should provide a two- to three-page synopsis of your proposal. Think of it as a *proposal in miniature*—it represents a short, private conversation that you are having with the decision makers. It's the first real component of your proposal. It follows immediately after the table of contents and precedes the first main proposal section.

You can probably trace the executive summary's origins to the huge proposals prepared for the federal government by defense and other types of contractors. The length of these proposals forced the contractors to summarize the main points of the proposal's content so that decision makers could get an idea of what they were about to read. The executive summary provided a heads-up to focus the proposal's recipients on the key points of the proposal.

Some people think an executive summary is unnecessary. They think it gives the buyer a way to avoid reading the entire proposal—they're right. Some proposal recipients will use the executive summary for just that purpose. But what would these recipients do if there were no executive summary; do you think they would feel obligated to read the entire proposal?

Your proposal's executive summary serves two critical purposes for your proposal's recipients:

- It provides some readers with a concise synopsis of your entire proposal, which alone probably makes the executive summary the single-most important component of your proposal.

- Many experienced decision makers read your proposal's executive summary expecting that it identifies the key issues discussed in your proposal's main body. The executive summary gives these readers a heads-up to the important issues presented in more detail in the main body of the sales proposal.

Think about it this way. An executive summary should be a *proposal in miniature.* It should capture the most important aspects of each of your proposal's five main sections and contain all the information that's needed to make an informed buying decision.

Writing it last

The executive summary represents a condensed version of your proposal. Logically, you can't write it until you finish writing the entire sales proposal. Actually, I've worked with some companies whose salespeople wrote their executive summaries first. They told us they used the executive summary as a blueprint for writing the rest of the proposal. Seems like strange logic—*let's summarize the proposal before we write it.*

Pretending that it's a miniature proposal

You are probably asking yourself "How do I take all the information on fifteen to twenty or more pages and boil it down to one or two pages? How can I possibly create a miniature proposal when everything in the proposal seems so important?" Actually, it can be easier than you think.

I'll assume that you wrote your proposal on a word-processing system. Simply just follow these steps:

1. Print a copy of your proposal.

2. Read each section and highlight, underline, or circle the most critical information in each section.

3. Save a copy of the proposal in a new file titled exec summary.

4. Using the new exec summary file, go through each section and delete everything except the critical information that you identified in the second step. Condense, condense, and then condense some more until you summarize each section in a couple of paragraphs.

5. Combine the paragraphs into your executive summary.

6. As an option, you may want to use the proposal's main section titles to create subsection titles in your executive summary.

7. Copy and paste the exec summary file into your proposal.

If you follow these steps a few times, you'll get to the point where you can write a top-notch executive summary in just a few minutes. Of course, that's assuming you start with a top-notch proposal.

If your company uses a proposal production system, it might be possible to generate the executive summary automatically; however, one must design a proposal model correctly and have a system with certain functional capabilities. Using our proposal production system, Sales Document Builder, we design proposal models that include executive summaries that are automatically generated with the proposal. This certainly eliminates a tedious task for the sales professionals.

Keeping it short: remember, it's supposed to be a summary

If you could write a *perfect* executive summary, it would be one page long. However, writing a one-page executive summary is very difficult, especially if the proposal is long and covers complex topics. Expect that your executive summaries will be two or three pages. The executive summary's page length is probably somewhat proportional to your proposal's page length. However, there are no hard and fast rules.

Use the same page format and layout in your executive summary that you used in the rest of the proposal. If the main sections of your proposal use lots of white space, which makes them easy to read, then your executive summary should have lots of white space too. Remember that you want to have an executive summary that's easy to read. Don't try to squeeze the executive summary on to one page by using a tiny font.

The following example is an executive summary from one of our company's (SalesProposals.com) sales proposal models. Notice that it has five subsections, one for each of the proposal's main sections. This example covers two 8.5" x 11" pages. Put yourself on the buyer's side of the desk as you read the example. Once again, pretend you're a decision maker.

Executive Summary

A sales proposal doesn't have to be good, just PERFECT!

Background Information

During our analysis, we identified critical business issues within the sales and proposal development processes for ABC Corporation:

- ABC sales proposals lack consistency and quality because sales professionals write their own proposals, which typically require three to four hours.
- The close ratio for ABC proposals is 25% because they are not customer focused and contain few compelling reasons for buyers to make a change.

We also identified important needs related to these critical business issues:

- Develop proposal models and other sales tools that will ensure consistency and quality of all sales proposals.
- Integrate the sales proposal production process with a customer relationship management (CRM) system when it is implemented next year.

Some important key pain indicators we defined for ABC Corporation's current sales and proposal development processes include:

- Number of proposals written annually: 400
- Number or proposals closed annually: 100
- Current proposal close ratio: 25%
- Estimated average cost to write one proposal: $225

Proposed SalesProposals.com Solution

SalesProposals.com proposes a consulting engagement for ABC Corporation to:

- Design and development of three (3) proposal models.
- Implement Sales Document Builder, its Web-based proposal and document automation system.

The proposed solution offers several benefits not easily measured in financial terms. The new ABC sales proposal models will:

- Provide a consistent, branded sales message for the company.

- Reinforce the company's consultative sales process by requiring sales professionals to ask critical questions and gather and process pertinent customer information.
- Differentiate ABC from its competition.
- Maximize the concept that ABC provides exceptional business and advanced widget solutions.
- Position the sale as the correct business solution and strategy.

The new sales proposal models and implementing Sales Document Builder should enable ABC Corporation immediately to boost profitability by increasing the company's *Proposal Close Ratio* to an estimated 27.5%. The higher close ratio will:

- Increase first year revenues by $1,000,000
- Provide an ROI of 667%

Reducing the time needed to produce custom sales proposals with the automated proposal generation capabilities of Sales Document Builder will:

- Reduce first year proposal production costs by $56,800
- Provide an ROI of 171%

Implementation

SalesProposals.com follows a phased approach to design and develop sales proposal models and implement Sales Document Builder (SDB). Each phase includes defined activities and deliverables. A team comprised of ABC Corporation and SalesProposals.com staff will complete the activities in six to seven weeks. SalesProposals.com is prepared to start the project on October 17, 2008.

SalesProposals.com Profile

SalesProposals.com specializes in sales proposal design, development, integration, and automation of winning, customer-focused sales proposals. Bob Kantin, the founder, has written several books on designing winning sales proposals and integrating them into a consultative sales process.

Two key reasons that make SalesProposals.com and Sales Document Builder the right choice for ABC Corporation are:

- SPC provides ABC with the two key components needed for a successful project: consulting resources to design and develop winning, customer-focused sales proposals and an Internet-based proposal production and management system.

> • Sales Document Builder, SPC's Web-based production and management system, will provide the required management oversight needed to monitor all ongoing production activities.
>
> **Costs and Commitments**
>
> SalesProposals.com fees to provide Sales Document Builder (SDB) and consulting services are.
>
> • Total consulting services fees: $15,000
> • SDB Startup fee: $ 2,000
> • Annual Sales Document Builder fees: $13,200

Now that you have finished reading the executive summary example, answer these questions:

- Does the executive summary give you a heads-up for what to expect in the rest of the proposal?

- Do you understand the important business issues and needs facing ABC relative to its sales and proposal development processes?

- Do you understand what SalesProposals.com is proposing for ABC?

- Do you think the financial benefits will create sufficient interest for a decision maker to want to read further?

Following Transmittal Letter Guidelines

Include a transmittal letter when sending or delivering your proposal—it's good business etiquette. Think of the transmittal letter as your proposal's cover letter. Address it to your primary contact or internal sponsor or whoever requested the proposal in the buyer's organization. Even though you address the letter to only one person, you can include a copy of the transmittal letter in every proposal so that all the decision makers have an opportunity to read it.

The components of a transmittal letter

Your transmittal letter needs to cover a lot of ground in no more than one page. Use it to:

- Tell why you're submitting the proposal to the buyer.

- Highlight the buyer's most critical business issues and explain that implementing your proposed solution will reduce or avoid costs, or increase revenues.

- Explain why your company is a good choice (summarize the *Why Us?* subsection from section three).

- Include an offer to provide additional information or assistance if requested by the buyer.

- Thank your contact for his or her time and efforts in helping you gather and define the information needed to write the proposal.

Besides using your best writing skills while writing a transmittal letter, you need to follow three guidelines. Your transmittal letter should be:

- No more than one page long

- Printed on company letterhead

- Signed by the sales professional who's responsible for the sale

Stuff to Remember

Ashley volunteered to write the executive summary. She said writing it didn't need to be a team effort. After all, nothing in the executive summary was going to be new—it was going represent the most important content extracted from their proposal model's five main sections.

The team agreed that their transmittal letters shouldn't read like a form or boilerplate letter. They felt that their transmittal letters should contain some required content but be customized for each client and their contact. Scott volunteered to draft a model for everyone to use.

√ A transmittal letter can help focus your proposal's readers because it:

- Gives your reasons for presenting the proposal
- Highlights the buyer's critical issues and your proposed solution

√ Your transmittal letter should be:

- No more than one page long
- Printed on company stationery
- Signed by the responsible sales professional

√ An executive summary also can focus your proposal's readers because it captures the essence of your proposal by:

- Providing summary information on all the key points contained within the proposal
- Alerting readers to the critical information contained in the proposal's main sections

√ Follow these guidelines when writing an executive summary:

- Write it last.
- Pretend that it's a miniature proposal.
- Keep it short.

11

Other Important Proposal Components and Packaging

"You're getting pretty smart," was Johnny's comment after the team had designed the proposal's executive summary and transmittal letter in record time. Ashley had taken the executive summary component as her project because all the guys thought it would be the most difficult. Her presentation had been straightforward and simple, "The executive summary is a proposal in miniature. To write one correctly, all we have to do is condense the proposal down to a few pages." That turned out to be a lot easier than she and the team had ever imagined.

Scott had taken the transmittal letter as his project. He had learned that a transmittal letter is simply the term used to describe the cover letter for the proposal. The team quickly saw how the proposal's transmittal letter also could be used to comment on some of the activities they completed as part of their sales process. The team spent less than forty minutes reviewing Scott's draft and creating a model for everyone to follow.

Now they were on to the three remaining components: title page, table of contents, and appendices. How tough could they be? After all, everyone understood the cover page and table of contents. Weren't appendices were just some add-on things that were stuck in the back of the proposal?

Johnny was interested to see what the other team members had learned while researching their components. He suspected they were about to learn more about these components than they realized.

This chapter discusses the last three proposal components that you need to consider while designing your proposal:

- Title page
- Table of contents
- Appendices

Treat these three components as the finishing touches to your proposal's structure and content. Pay attention to detail on these three components to ensure your proposal projects a professional image.

Creating a Title Page

Think of your proposal's title page like it's the cover to a book. The title page conveys some basic information:

- Buyer's name
- Proposal's title
- Submission date
- Seller's name (and, as an option, address)
- Seller's logo, if it has one

Here's another tip: ask marketing for some help. They usually have creative people who can create very professional-looking graphics. You'll be surprised how big a difference a top-notch cover page will make for your proposal.

One of our clients, Bombardier Flexjet, sells fractional ownership of corporate aircraft. Working with Flexjet's project team, we designed what we thought was an attractive cover page for their proposal models complete with the ability to select one of five pictures for the cover page when they generated a proposal from Sales Document Builder, our automated production system. Flexjet has a creative marketing group and also uses an external ad agency. After seeing our title page, they asked if they could change the layout. In short order, marketing and the ad agency redesigned the title page. It wasn't too much different; however, it certainly created a much more professional-looking first impression.

Be careful using the buyer's logo

You can include the buyer's logo on the title page of your proposal. But be careful. You first should get permission from the buyer before using its logo. Some organizations don't want anyone reproducing their logos.

In fact, you need to tread cautiously even if your contact with the buyer says that using its logo is all right. He may not be aware of some marketing department policy that restricts use of its logo. What do you think would happen if the vice president of marketing got a copy of your proposal?

What's in a title?

Most companies don't spend much time thinking about their proposals' title. Don't use a bland sales proposal title like everyone else does. If you're selling electric widgets, don't title your proposal "Electric Widgets Proposal." Be a bit creative. A more interesting title that can really focus the reader's attention might be "Increasing Employee Accuracy by Installing Electric Widgets." Think about this example. Without knowing anything about the proposal's content, this more interesting title does two things for the reader, it identifies:

- The buyer's critical business issue—the need to raise employee accuracy levels

- A key benefit of installing electric widgets—a way to increase employee accuracy

Here's another example. An employee testing company, eSelect.com, can use either of these titles for its proposal:

- "Increasing Employee Retention through Personality Profile Testing"

- "eSelect.com Personality Profile Testing Proposal"

Both titles are appropriate. But which one do you think is more effective? See how titling your proposal can make a difference?

To create a great title for you proposal, just answer a few questions and then combine your answers into a title:

- What's the buyer's most critical business issue?

- What's the primary benefit of installing our product?

- What are you proposing?

Using the correct names and submission date

Put the buyer's name and your name on the title page. This isn't too difficult. Simply follow these rules:

* Use the full name of both the buying and selling companies.

* For individuals, use first names, middle initials, and last names.

* Don't use nicknames, abbreviations, or acronyms.

The date that you formally present your proposal to the buyer should be the submission date. Follow two simple guidelines:

* The submission date on the title page and the date on your transmittal letter should be the same.

* Write out the month, day, and year; do not use a numerical date. For example, October 17, 2008, rather than 10/17/08 or 10-17-2008.

Including a Table of Contents

Your proposal's table of contents provides a roadmap or blueprint for the reader. A proposal's table of contents has two purposes, it:

* Shows readers how your proposal is organized

* Helps the reader locate particular information in your proposal, which can be very helpful to the reader after he has read your proposal and wants to reread some section

At a minimum, the table of contents should list the titles and page numbers for the:

* Executive summary

* Main sections

* All the subsections within each main section

* Appendices

Follow these simple rules when numbering pages in your proposal:

* All the pages in your proposal need a number except the title page.

- Optionally, use Roman numerals for the table of contents and the executive summary—it really is more correct than having your table of contents as page one (1). The first page of the table of contents is page i.

- Number the pages in the five main sections one after the other; the first page of the first proposal section is page 1.

- You have two options for numbering the pages of your appendices. You can:

    - Continue numbering from the proposal's main sections

    - Use each appendix's alphabetic designation as part of the page number; the third page of Appendix C would be C-3. Do whichever is easier.

Automating your table of contents

If you're using a word-processing system to write your proposal, you can probably automatically generate a table of contents. If you use Microsoft Word, you can automate your table of contents by assigning paragraph *Heading* styles (Heading 1, Heading 2, Heading 3, etc.) to section and subsection titles.

Enter "table of contents" in the *Help* program function and follow the simple steps. It's not magic or rocket science—your table of contents will automatically appear. More important, you can automatically update your table of contents at anytime.

Including Appendices

Appendices can make it easier for you to design and write your sales proposal by:

- Helping you maintain your proposal's flow of information and ideas by giving you a way to reduce the amount of detail in the main sections. In other words, appendices help you control the length of the main sections.

- Offering a convenient way to include preprinted materials that you need to show the buyer. You can put brochures, product specifications, cost analyses, and so on in appendices rather than in the main section of your proposal.

Maintaining the flow

A well-written sales proposal should hold the reader's attention with its flow of information and ideas. You need to provide enough detail in the main sections to support key points; however, you never want to include too much or extraneous information because you risk overloading the reader. Too much detail can be confusing or dull. It may bore some readers to the point where they miss the critical reasons why their company needs to make a change.

Putting preprinted materials in appendices

You ruin the professional appearance of your proposal by putting preprinted materials in the main body. Putting preprinted materials in your proposal interrupts its flow of information and ideas. If you think there's a need to put something like a brochure or a specifications sheet in the middle of your proposal, you probably want the reader to read some critical information in the document. Give the reader a break. She will really appreciate it if you summarized the information on the preprinted material that you want her to read rather than sticking the complete brochure or spec sheet in your proposal. Write one or two paragraphs telling her what she needs to know and put the preprinted material in an appendix.

One of my first sales proposal consulting clients wanted to insert a product specification sheet in the middle of the "Proposed Solution" section of their proposal. The VP of sales was adamant about doing this. He felt that if they were proposing the product, then a decision maker would want to closely study the spec sheet to make sure it would deliver exactly what they needed.

I needed to convince my client that the spec sheet belonged in the proposal but not in the main body. Here's the logic that I used:

- I asked if all of their proposal recipients would know what to look for or would understand most of the information on the spec sheet. The VP of sales conceded that some of the decision makers might know little about the meaning of many of the product specifications.

- Then, I asked him to identify which of the product's functions clearly differentiated their product from the competition. He readily identified four or five that he said were unique in the industry.

- Next, I asked him to identify the most important features of the product and list the benefits each provides (which were not on the spec sheet).

- Finally, I then told him the appearance and format of the proposal and spec sheet were different and that we needed a consistent look and feel. Did he want the proposal to look more like the spec sheet or the spec sheet to look like the proposal?

He finally got it. We created a "Proposed Solution" section that described the product, defined its application for the buyer, identified its main functions, and listed its features and benefits. One sentence in the section read, "For more details, see Appendix B: Product Specifications."

Following two guidelines about appendices

Use these two simple guidelines when developing appendices for your proposals:

- **No dangling appendices.** Don't put an appendix in the back of your proposal unless you reference it in one of the main proposal sections. If you have an appendix in your proposal that's not referenced in a main section, you're just wasting paper and probably confusing the readers.

- **Follow the order of reference.** Put your appendices in the same order that they're referenced in the main proposal. For example, the first referenced appendix becomes Appendix A, the next referenced appendix becomes Appendix B, and so forth. This guideline is really just common sense.

Using some common appendices

Table 11-1 can give you ideas on how to correctly use some common appendices in your proposals. In the table, I use the term *biographical* resume. A biographical resume lists work experience and education, but it omits phone numbers, addresses, and so on.

Table 11-1 Common Appendices

Appendix	Comments
ROI Valuation	Put an explanation of the key pain indicators and critical assumptions used in the ROI valuation and the summarized numbers in the financial benefits subsection. Put a complete copy of the supporting analysis in an appendix.
Biographical Resumes	Keep the main proposal short; only list names and titles in the proposal. Use a standard format for all biographical resumes; try to keep the length equal for all resumes.
Implementation or Project Methods	Put major project or engagement phases, activities, and deliverables in the proposal. Use an appendix to provide detail or list all activities. You may also want to use a bar chart in the proposal.
Customer List	Unless you really think it's important, don't put your entire list of customer or client names in the proposal. Use an appendix for a complete customer list. Make sure that it's okay to include the customer or client name on the list. Don't confuse your customer or client list with your customer references subsection in section four.

Stuff to Remember

Johnny's team quickly agreed upon the content and layout of the proposal's title page with some help from marketing. They decided that the table of contents should include main sections, the subsections within a main section, and appendices. Finally, they listed the proposal model's appendices in the order that they were referenced in the proposal. They also decide two appendices would be optional at a sales professional's discretion.

√ Think of your proposal's title page like it's the cover to a book. A top-notch cover page will differentiate your proposal. Create a title that includes the buyer's most important critical business issue and the primary benefit of what you're proposing.

√ Your proposal's table of contents provides a roadmap or blueprint for the reader. It should provide page numbers for the proposals: executive summary, main sections and subsections, and appendices.

√ Appendices can make it easier for you to design and write your sales proposal by: 1) giving you a way to reduce the amount of detail in the main sections and 2) offering a convenient way to include preprinted materials.

12

Creating a Quality Look and Feel for the Proposal

The final product was very impressive. Johnny thought his team had done an exceptional job designing their new sales proposal model. Everyone thought it had a logical structure with all the right information. Scott said it would help them close more business because it was doubly focused; first it was buyer-focused—designed from the viewpoint of the buyer's decision makers. And second, it was seller-focused—its information requirements would help them gather and define the appropriate buyer information.

Ashley raised another issue. She said, "This proposal model represents the best any of us have ever written, but it just doesn't look like a winner. We need to think about the first impression its appearance gives the reader." Some team members didn't understand what Ashley was talking about. They thought the proposal looked just fine—after all, they weren't graphic artists. Others agreed with Ashley—the proposal's general appearance needed some help.

Johnny said, "Let's table this discussion for a few days. I'm going to show our model to Sara, the director of corporate marketing, and ask her for some help and ideas."

Most of this book covers the substance of your proposal. This chapter covers form—the physical look and feel of the proposal. You want to make your proposal attractive and engaging by:

- Selecting font styles for headings and text
- Designing tables and illustrations of various kinds

- Choosing a binding method

If you do this job right, you can create a real *page turner,* as they say in book publishing. Your proposal can be interesting and informative. More important, it can be very persuasive.

Making Sure It's the Right Font

Selecting the correct fonts for the narrative and headings of your proposal is important because the right font makes your proposal easy to read and gives it a professional appearance. You may be more familiar with the terms *type* or *typeface* instead of *font.* All three terms are (more or less) interchangeable and refer to the way that letters and numbers look.

Ask for some help from others within your company if you're not sure what fonts look good or make sense. Start with the marketing department. You may find that it has selected the font for everyone in the company to use on all documents. Although they may be surprised that you're asking for help, once they realize why you're asking, they can probably show you exactly how to get a certain look in your sales proposals.

If your company doesn't have a marketing department, grab one of your company's latest brochures. Look at the different fonts used in the brochure and decide if the same fonts can work in your sales proposal. If your company doesn't have brochures, study as many brochures from other companies as you can. Pay close attention to how the brochures use and combine different fonts.

If you're still struggling with font matters and your company doesn't have a company look that you can follow, pick one or two familiar fonts and stick with them. I suggest Times New Roman or Garamond for the text and Arial for major headings (see examples in Figure 12-1).

Warning: Don't use some oddball font that only three people in the Western Hemisphere have ever seen. Doing so will only distract readers from your proposal's content.

More about fonts

You should know the difference between *serif* and *sans serif* fonts. Serifs are those tiny lines that cross the ending strokes of most characters (the font used for the main text in this book has serifs). Serifs have an important job: They help the reader's eye move easily along the line, which makes reading easier and more efficient.

Sans serif font, font without serifs, works well for major titles and section and subsection names. Check any of the chapter titles and subheadings in this book for an example of sans serif font. Figure 11-1 also has examples of serif and sans serif font styles.

One more thing about type is that a type's height determines its size. Type size is expressed in units called *points*. One point equals 1/72 inch. You probably want to use 10 to 12 point for proposal text, 12 point or larger for subsection names, and 14 or larger for section names.

Figure 12-1 Arial is a Sans Serif Font and All the Other Type Styles Have Serifs (in this figure)

Arial Bold, 14 pt for section headings
(Heading 1)

Arial Bold, 12 pt for subsection headings (Heading 2)

Arial Bold Italic, 10 pt for subsection headings (Heading 3)

Times New Roman, 12 pt, book weight for proposal text

Garamond, 12 pt book weight for proposal text

Time New Roman, 10 pt, book weight for proposal text

Garamond, 10 pt book weight for proposal text

Laying Out the Pages

Take some time to lay out your proposal so that its sections, subsections, tables, and other elements work together for easy reading. In particular *do not* use:

- Full text pages, which are simply pages of text from top to bottom. They make your proposal difficult to read. Instead use bullets, tables, and white space, which means not filling the page with text.

- Elaborate headers and footers because they distract from your proposal's message.

Figures 12-2 and 12-3 show how attention to formatting helps reveal the content of a proposal. Figure 12-2 is a plain page. It uses a serif type for text and a sans serif type for section and subsection headings. This page contains lots of information. Figure 12-3 contains the same information and uses the same types for text and headings; it uses bulleted lists to help the reader focus on important information.

Figure 12-2 Full Page of Text—Difficult and Boring for the Reader

Background Information: ABC Mortgage

ABC Mortgage is the largest mortgage loan origination company in Ohio with more than 12 years of mortgage lending experience. The company has twenty branch offices system in Ohio. ABC has more than 220 experienced mortgage professionals who closed nearly $1 billion in home loans in 2006, up from $860 million in 2005.

Current Loan Documentation Systems and Processes

ABC uses the Newton Loan Origination System. It archives its documents in in-house vaults and at the Iron Tunnel offsite storage.

Key Pain Indicators

During our analysis, we also identified current key pain indicators for ABC Mortgage Company.

Last year ABC processed 2,000 loans. The calculated current annual cost for loan origination processing personnel is $857,500. Further, we determined that the annual current cost for personnel searching for loan documentation is $24,811. ABC has 21,000 loan files stored at various locations. The calculated annual cost for storage of loan documentation is $36,243.

Issues and Impacts

We defined several issues with the current loan documentation systems and processes. Most important, the physical storage capacity is nearing its limits. Loan processing and servicing is overly reliant on moving and accessing paper.

These issues are impacting the organization. ABC understands that the use of valuable floor space for document storage is an inefficient. It also realizes that the continued dependence on paper movement to support loan processing and servicing activities places lower limits of the per capita throughput than can be achieved through image processing.

Goals

During our analysis we identified several goals ABC Mortgage Company has for improving its loan documentation systems and processes. It wants to avoid build-out cost and free storage space in the main building for other uses. More importantly the space issue, ABC wants to increase processing efficiencies through the integration of image technology with existing systems.

Figure 12-3 Reformatted Figure 12-2 — *Easier to Read*

Background Information: ABC Mortgage

ABC Mortgage is the largest mortgage loan origination company in Ohio with more than 12 years of mortgage lending experience. The company has twenty branch offices system in Ohio. ABC has more than 220 experienced mortgage professionals who closed nearly $1 billion in home loans in 2006, up from $860 million in 2005.

Current Loan Documentation Systems and Processes

- Loan origination system: Newton Loan Origination System
- Document archiving: In-house vaults and Iron Tunnel offsite storage

Key Pain Indicators

During our analysis, we also identified these current key pain indicators for ABC Mortgage Company:

- Number of loans that will be processed this year: 2,000
- Calculated current annual cost for loan origination processing personnel: $857,500
- Annual current cost for personnel searching for loan documentation: $24,811
- Number of loan files stored at various locations: 21,000
- Calculated annual cost for storage of loan documentation: $36,243

Issues and Impacts

We defined several issues with the current loan documentation systems and processes:
- Physical storage capacity is nearing its limits.
- Loan processing and servicing is overly reliant on moving and accessing paper.

We also defined the impact these issues have on the organization:
- Use of valuable floor space for document storage is an inefficient use of space.
- Continued dependence on paper movement to support loan processing and servicing activities places lower limits of the per capita throughput than can be achieved through image processing.

Goals

During our analysis we identified several goals ABC Mortgage Company has for improving its loan documentation systems and processes.
- Avoid build-out cost and free storage space in the main building for other uses.
- Increase processing efficiencies through the integration of image technology with existing systems.

If you had to read an entire proposal and could pick its format and layout, would you pick the first or the second example? What if the reader needed to find some specific fact, which would be easier? *Note:* This is an actual example from one of our client's proposals.

Using Pictures, Graphics, Tables, and Charts

If you're proficient with your word processing software, you can easily add pictures and graphics to your proposals. You can also create useful tables and charts right in your word processing system. You probably don't need to hire a graphic artist to add some interest to your sales proposals.

The much-used phrase, "a picture is worth a thousand words," certainly applies to sales proposals. You can convey a lot of information about your product by adding a few pictures or graphics. For example, several of our software clients use screen shots with callouts in their proposals to illustrate key functions of their systems. Others include such things as aircraft floor plans, data flow diagrams, and pictures of key product components.

Putting information in tables and charts will add to your proposal's readability. As you'll see in some examples, tables and charts also help you effectively and efficiently communicate complex information and ideas. Besides, both can make your proposal more interesting and enhance your message.

Put it in a table

Use tables in your proposals to display numbers and words in rows and columns. Tables are normally too complicated for a reader to just glance at in order to understand their messages. Consider using tables to condense and organize information so it's easier for readers to understand and comprehend.

Figure 12-4 shows how a fictitious software vendor, Digitalistics, proposes to convert a mortgage bank's manual document processing operation to its data processing system. The table defines the activities and deliverables in each phase of the conversion.

It doesn't contain all the conversion tasks and activities, but the level of detail in this table is probably more than adequate for most decision makers. Tables like this can reduce the risk some decision makers associate with making a change.

Figure 12-4 Implementation Activities in a Table

Phase	Activities	Deliverables
Project Kickoff	• Team introductions • Define Team member roles and responsibilities • Establish project contacts • Define project needs	• Required Project Needs • Preliminary timeline • Contact Information
Discovery	• Investigation and confirmation of Functional Requirements • Finalize Implementation Plan	• Functional Requirements • Implementation Plan
Design and Develop Required Functionality	• Design/Develop Components: - Software - Hardware - Telecom • Develop Internal System Test Plan • Co develop User Acceptance Test Plan with Client	• Hardware/Telecom ordering information • User Acceptance Test Plan • Internal System Test Plan
Build Out	• Hardware installed (dual-site) • Database setup • Software Component Unit Testing	• Hardware installed • Telecom requirements installed
System Testing	• Digitalistics Internal System testing	• Preparation for client User Acceptance Testing
User Acceptance Testing	• Client Training • Develop Training Plan • Client performs User Acceptance Testing with support of Digitalistics	• Training Plan • User Acceptance Test completed
Client Readiness	• Digitalistics supported Client User Training	• Trained Client user community
Production Cutover	• Digitalistics Client production signoff • Digitalistics Turnover to Production and Customer Care	• Fully functional production environment

Use charts to communicate, compare, and add interest

Use charts in your proposal to communicate relationships of parts to a whole, changes over time, and compare amounts. Charts also add visual interest to your proposal.

Think about this. When we first started reading, there were lots of pictures in our books. As we got older there were fewer pictures. Perhaps adding charts to your proposals will appeal to the decision makers' inner child. You have to ask a psychologist if that will help you sell more, but I think it sure sounds pretty impressive in a book on sales proposals.

There are three types of charts to consider:

- **Pie charts.** Your readers can absorb the message in one glance if it's in a pie chart. Use pie charts to show the approximate relationship of the parts to a whole. For example, you can use a pie chart to show the types of investments in a customer's portfolio, the distribution of ages in a buyer's employee population, or illustrate market share within the buyer's industry. But if you want the reader to compare data or understand precise differences, use a bar chart or line chart.

- **Line charts.** Use a line chart to illustrate changes over time. The vertical axis represents quantity and the horizontal axis represents time. For example, if your proposal needs to show your buyer's increased costs over the last several years, you could use a line chart. The vertical axis on your table would represent costs and the horizontal axis would represent time.

- **Bar charts.** Use bar charts in your proposals if you want to compare amounts. You can use vertical or horizontal bars to represent amounts and the sections or lines to designate quantity units. You can also use bar charts to compare different things or to show changes over time. For example, you can use a bar chart in the implementation section to communicate your project's or engagement's planned schedule. Or you can use a bar chart to compare the number of customers you have to the number that your competitors have.

Figure 12-5 shows how you can use a bar chart (or Gantt chart) to graphically communicate activities over time.

Figure 12-5 Gantt Chart Example

Phase	Week	1	2	3	4	5	6	7	8	9	10
Project Kickoff		■									
Discovery			▨								
Design/Development				■	■	■					
Build Out					▨	▨	▨				
System Testing								■			
User Acceptance Testing									▨		
Client Readiness										■	
Production Cutover											▨

Ensuring Quality Reproduction

Printing your proposal shouldn't be an issue. You can purchase laser and inkjet printers for prices that range from less than $100 to several thousand dollars for high-speed, high-resolution color printers. Even the least expensive laser or inkjet printer produces quality output.

Add some color

Your word processing system lets you add color to your sales proposals, which adds to its appearance and readability. Color can do more than decorate pages; it can help communicate your message to the reader. You can use two, or possibly three, text colors for the sake of contrast. For example, you could use colored section and subsection titles to help the reader visually organize and categorize information. If possible, use color in your tables and charts to make them easier to understand.

Don't go overboard by using too many text colors, because an abundance of colors can slow readers down or make your message harder to understand and remember. Check with your marketing department. They may have defined standard brand colors for the company.

Paper is important

One of the easiest and least costly ways to add to quality is by upgrading the paper you use for your proposals. Most printers and plain paper photocopiers can handle any grade, surface, or weight of paper, except for some high-gloss, coated papers. You might think about getting special paper for your proposals. For example, you might want to get paper that has your company's logo as a watermark.

Don't use standard 20# paper. At a minimum, use 24# bond paper for your proposals.

Dividing a Proposal into Bite-sized Pieces

Use section dividers or tabs in your proposals. Dividers are a low-cost way to make your proposal stand out in the crowd because they:

- Enhance your proposal's appearance
- Add readability to your proposal because they help readers separate, categorize, and find information
- Make a long proposal seem shorter

For example, if your proposal is thirty-five pages long and you don't use dividers, readers may think it's a lot to read. After all, they're staring at a big stack of paper. But if you use dividers, you cut the pile into bite-size pieces (probably four to five pages a bite).

Use dividers to separate the proposal's table of contents, executive summary, and the five main sections. If you use appendices in your proposals, use a divider to separate each appendix.

Using preprinted dividers

If all your proposals use the same main section names, then you can use preprinted dividers. However, if main section names change from one proposal to the next, use a copy center or other resource during the proposal's duplication process that has the ability to print and insert custom dividers.

Some more guidelines for dividers

If you decide to use dividers in your proposals, you need to know the details on what type of dividers to use. Don't use dividers that:

- Extend beyond the proposal's cover because it looks cheap and creates the impression of poor quality
- Are inexpensive and require you to type titles onto little pieces of paper

Try to use dividers that have a plastic or color coating to increase their durability and enhance your proposal's appearance. Also, make sure the font on your dividers matches a font used within your proposal. Doing so enhances your proposal's overall appearance.

Tip: If you use preprinted tab dividers, you add several pages to your proposal. You can leave these pages blank or you can ask marketing to help you design some graphics for each divider.

Binding and Covering a Proposal

Finally, you're ready to package your proposal. If you've been designing your proposal as you're reading this book, you have the look that you want. Now you need to put it in a nice package for the buyer. Packaging is important because your buyer will partially judge your proposal by its cover—by how it's packaged.

Stapling doesn't get it

Never simply staple your proposals in the upper-left corner. Staples are not a binding option for sales proposals. Luckily, you have several easy and inexpensive binding options: wire, perfect, GBC, three-ring, and others. Some of these binding options you can use in-house. Other binding options may require you to go to a copy center or printer. Visit your local office supply store, copy center, and printer to select the best binding option for your proposals. When you select a binding option, keep in mind that your proposal's binding should be:

- Convenient for the proposal's reader
- Durable

Binding options may determine cover options

Obviously, the binding option you select may determine which cover options are available for your proposals. For example, if you use three-ring binders, your proposal's cover will be...a three-ring binder. Keep in mind that you can get three-ring binders with preprinted covers. Preprinted covers in your company's colors and with your company's logo can enhance the overall appearance of your proposal. Hey, if you use preprinted covers for your proposal, the buyer might assume that your company is stable and has been around for a long time. So, pick a binding option that allows you to use preprinted covers.

One of our client's packages its proposals in three-ring, simulated-leather binders embossed with its logo. It also uses preprinted dividers with product graphics displayed on each. This client uses lots of color including color photographs in its proposals. The cost to produce each proposal probably exceeds $50; however, its proposals can range in value from $500,000 to $20 million. The client's rationale for such a high proposal packaging cost is this: *What difference does it make if we spend $400 to provide all the decision makers with one of our proposals? If it helps us close a deal worth at a minimum $500,000, it's worth every dollar!*

Giving Every Decision Maker the Very Best

Always ask your contact or internal sponsor in the buyer's organization this question: "How many copies of the proposal will you need?" You want to make sure that every decision maker gets an original proposal; in other words, don't give a "very best" copy to your prime contact and sub-par versions to everyone else.

The last thing you want to have happen is to have the buyer make copies of your proposal, staple the copies in the upper-left corner, and distribute the copies to the decision makers. What do you think will happen to your proposal's carefully crafted, high-quality look if your contact makes cheap copies for the decision makers? For a few extra dollars you can send the very best to every one of the buyer's decision makers. You can't afford not to!

Stuff to Remember

The director of corporate marketing was amazing. In a few hours she showed Johnny how to take his above-average proposal and turn it into a show-stopper. Sara first told Johnny how to correctly use the corporate standard fonts. She changed some page layouts and added color. She was so impressed with the proposal's structure and content that she designed a custom binder and divider tabs. More important for Johnny, she agreed to pay the production costs.

When Johnny showed his team the final proposal model and told them about the custom binders and divider tabs, they were ecstatic. Everyone agreed that they all would make quota this year. Johnny said, "Because of the new proposals, I'm raising everyone's quota 25 percent—just kidding."

√ The physical look and feel of your proposal is important because you want to make your proposal attractive and engaging.

√ Select the correct fonts for the narrative and headings of your proposal because they make your proposal easy to read and give it a professional appearance.

√ Take some time to lay out your proposal so that its sections, subsections, tables, and other elements work together. In particular, don't use full text pages. Instead use bullets, tables, and white space.

√ Putting information in tables and charts will add to your proposal's readability.

√ Color adds to your proposal's appearance and readability; color can help communicate your message to the reader.

√ At a minimum, use 24# bond paper for your proposals.

√ Dividers enhance your proposal's appearance, add readability, and make a long proposal seem shorter.

√ Packaging is important because your buyer will partially judge your proposal by its cover—by how it's packaged.

√ Make sure that every decision maker gets an original proposal.

13

Using a Letter Proposal—
When Smaller is Better

Ashley told Johnny that she was working on a small deal for an existing client and felt that their new twenty-plus page proposal was more than was needed for this buyer and deal. She wanted to send more than a one- or two-page price quote, because she still had to sell the deal to the buyer's decision makers—she wasn't just taking an order. Ashley thought she needed something in between a price quote and the detailed proposal.

Over the next few days, Johnny talked with other members of his team. Some were questioning why Ashley didn't want to use their new proposal model, because it was helping everyone win business. Others agreed with Ashley, they too would like a smaller version of the new proposal to use for follow-up on business with existing customers or for small deals with new customers.

Johnny wasn't ready to initiate another project to design a smaller version of their new proposal model. But, he had to admit, a smaller proposal might have its place for some deals.

When you ask people what they think when you say the words sales proposals, many will say the first thing that comes to mind is a three-ring binder filled with pages of text, product specs, tables, and marketing hype. Some say that a proposal has to be long to be good. Others might say a proposal's length is tied to its value—the longer a proposal, the higher its dollar value. Still others might think that they have to write long proposals to sell a complex product. Or the complexity of a product or service application adds length to their proposals.

Here's an important announcement: *Not all proposals have to be long.* Many companies and professionals may find themselves in sales situations that call for smaller proposals. They find that a five- to ten-page proposal is long enough and that a letter format is very effective. These sales professionals write *letter proposals.*

Proposing in a Smaller Package

A letter proposal contains all the logic and content requirements of a regular, full-size proposal, just in a smaller package. The purpose of a letter proposal is the same as the large, standard proposal. You might think of a letter proposal fitting somewhere between an executive summary and a standard sales proposal. An executive summary is a proposal in miniature—it's a synopsis of the entire proposal. A standard sales proposal contains all the recommended sections and components: a transmittal letter, an executive summary, the five recommended main sections, and supporting appendices—a letter proposal is a hybrid.

Table 13-1 Standard versus Letter Proposal Content Comparison

Proposal Section or Component	Letter Proposal	Standard Proposal
Title page		x
Subject line	x	
Transmittal letter		x
Table of contents		x
Background information	x	x
Proposed solution	x	x
Implementation	x	x
Seller profile	x	x
Business considerations	x	x
Approval (section)	x	
Appendices (or attachments)	x	x

Table 13-1 compares the proposal sections and components contained in a letter proposal with those in a full-length, standard proposal. As you can see, a letter proposal contains the same information that you put in the five-section sales proposal. However, a letter proposal uses fewer pages to convey the message and the information.

Note: You can add appendices to a letter proposal to control its length, just like you use appendices with a full-sized proposal. However, you might use a different name—you can call them *attachments* rather than *appendices* in a letter proposal.

Deciding When to Use a Letter Proposal

Designing and writing letter proposals is easy if you think about the letter proposal as a shortened version of a standard proposal. You can use letter proposals the same way that you use regular proposals. And you should integrate your letter proposal development process into your consultative sales process.

Letter proposals may work well for you in one of the following sales situations:

- You're selling an uncomplicated product.

- The proposal has a low dollar value.

- The proposal is an add-on or small interim sale to an existing customer.

- The buyer only wants a simple proposal to document an understanding that they've reached with you.

One of our clients sells integrated security systems. Because their deals can range from less than $5,000 to $200,000+, we developed three types of proposals for its sales force:

- Formal, standard proposal for the big deals

- Letter proposal for follow on business to existing clients and mid-sized deals with new clients

- Letter proposal *express* for small deals to existing and new clients

Offering a Perfect Fit for Consultants

Letter proposals work perfectly for small consulting firms or independent consultants. Because your letter proposal is a condensed version of your standard proposal, you can easily educate the buyer on all aspects of its critical business issues, your proposed consulting services, and the benefits of your proposed engagement. Further, letter proposals work for small consulting firms and independent consultants because their deals are usually smaller in dollar terms and often not for a complex engagement with a staff of consultants.

Your buyers may find that a letter proposal doesn't seem to be as imposing as a standard proposal, even though your letter proposal's sales message should be just as compelling. Because a letter proposal is shorter, it's easier and faster to design and write. You can also add an acceptance section with signature lines to your letter proposal. This section makes approving your proposed engagement super-convenient. (I write about the acceptance section later in this chapter.)

For example, SalesProposals.com (SPC), my company, designs and develops sales proposal models and integrates their production into the client's sales process. Typical consulting engagements range from $10,000 to $30,000. Normally SPC uses letter proposals because of the length and size of the average engagement: short-term and small.

SPC also sells its Web-based proposal production system, Sales Document Builder (SDB). We use a full-length, standard proposal format for some of these larger contracts because they add the acquisition and implementation of SDB into the deal and typically include a training program for the client's sales force.

Condensing Content into a Letter Proposal

When you design and write a letter proposal, keep in mind that it's a standard proposal in letter format. Use the same flow of information and ideas that you use in your standard proposal—the same five proposal sections. For example, the first several paragraphs of a letter proposal contain the buyer background information normally found in section one of a standard proposal.

Here are some things to keep in mind because a letter proposal is short and in letter format:

* It doesn't need a table of contents.

* It's so short that you don't need an executive summary.

* You can include a section for buyer approval instead of a separate contract or purchase order.

Understanding Key Letter Proposal Components

Following are some key components you may want to include in your letter proposal.

Use the subject line for the title

Treat the subject line in your letter proposal like the title page of a standard proposal (see Chapter 11 to help you write a powerful title). Use it to link a buyer's critical business issue with your proposed product or service.

Include pieces of a transmittal letter

Put some key pieces of a transmittal letter at the beginning and end of your letter proposal. Start your letter proposal by explaining why you're submitting it to the buyer. And you can end your letter proposal by thanking your contact for his or her time and effort in helping you gather the information for the proposal.

Include the five proposal sections

Use the five standard proposal sections in your letter proposal. Try to reduce each section to less than one page, but don't be too surprised if one or two sections in your letter proposal are longer.

Get the buyer to sign in the proposal

Make it easy for the buyer to approve your proposal by putting an acceptance section in your letter proposal. Include a signature and date line for an authorized buyer representative to approve your proposal.

Note: Before you add an acceptance section to your letter proposal, get some legal advice. Your attorney may want you to add some legal wording to your letter proposal or your attorney may want you to attach a contract to your letter proposal.

Use attachments like appendices in a standard proposal

You can use attachments to control the length of your letter proposals, just like you use appendices with a standard proposal. Remember that length is critical. The maximum length of a letter proposal should be no more than ten or twelve pages. Therefore, if you need to put details in your letter proposal, summarize the information and put the detail in an attachment. Remember, in letter proposals you should probably use the term *attachment* rather than *appendix,* but they're the same thing.

Write a letter proposal like it's a business letter

Put the first page of your letter proposal on your company's standard business letterhead and use matching paper for all the other pages. Since it's in letter format, treat the letter proposal like you would a multiple-page letter. This means you need to put a page number on every page except the first.

Make your letter proposal easy to scan. Remember nobody reads anymore, they just scan. Here are some tips to make your letter proposal easy to scan, use:

- Lots of white space—no full pages of text
- Headings and subheadings
- Bulleted lists
- Tables and charts

Stuff to Remember

Johnny asked Ashley if she wanted to take a shot at developing a proposal in letter format using the deal with her client as the pilot test. They agreed the "Letter" proposal won't need the executive summary and all of the sections needed to be pared down. Johnny thought a six to eight page proposal would work.

Two days later, Ashley showed Johnny her first draft. He thought it was perfect. It truly was their big proposal model condensed to fit a smaller deal. Ashley said it really wasn't that much work once she realized it was mostly condensing and reformatting.

√ A letter proposal contains all the logic and content requirements of a regular, full-size proposal, just in a smaller package.

√ Not all proposals have to be long. Many sales situations call for smaller proposals:

- You're selling an uncomplicated product.

- The proposal has a low dollar value.

- The proposal is an add-on or small interim sale to an existing customer.

- The buyer only wants a simple proposal to document an understanding that they've reached with you.

14

Building a Custom Sales Proposal Development Process

Johnny knew and so did management that not everyone was closely following a consultative sales process. In reality there's no "company-approved" process that management endorses or supports. Everyone in sales, including his team members, tend to do their own thing. But now Johnny and his team have developed some very buyer-focused sales proposal models, which require rigorous and well-defined buyer information–gathering activities. So his sales team will have to sell consultatively or they won't be able to use their new proposals.

Johnny decided he and his team weren't finished with their proposal project. Their last task will be to identify the activities and sales tools that were going to comprise their sales proposal development process. Johnny wants to be sure his team members will be using the new proposal models correctly. Most important, he wants to guarantee a payback for all the time and effort they had spent on the project.

By the time you reach this chapter in the book, you know that the key to writing winning sales proposals is the integration of two processes: consultative selling and proposal development. Integrating your selling process with your proposal develop process may make sense to you; however, it may not to other people in your company. For example, sales professionals or senior management may not embrace the idea. If this is the case, you need to decide what it's going to take to integrate the processes. Answer the following questions to help you decide if your company is ready.

Question #1: Do your company's sales professionals follow a consultative sales process? Yes or No

This is an important question, so carefully consider your response. Answering these related, secondary questions should help decide your answer to Question #1.

	Yes	No
• Have all the sales professionals attended formal consultative sales training?	___	___
• Does sales management constantly support and reinforce the sales process?	___	___
• Has sales training been customized for your company and its products or services?	___	___
• Does the sales process incorporate custom sales tools for the sales professionals, e.g., process letters, ROI valuation tools, etc.?	___	___
• Does the sales process have clearly defined phases with sales activities within each phase that everyone follows?	___	___

If you answered "Yes" to four or more of these questions, your sales professionals most likely are selling consultatively; you can answer "Yes" to question #1 and go to the next question.

If you answered "No" to two or more of the related questions, your answer to this question #1 is "No." Obviously not all of your sales professionals are selling consultatively. For example, some companies just send new hires to a public sales training seminar and expect they will magically become consultative sales professionals. This action doesn't guarantee success especially if management does actively support the process.

Further, if you answered "No" to this first question, you have gaps in your sales organization and may have a major problem. You want the company's sales proposals to be buyer-focused, but your sales professionals aren't selling consultatively. Before your sales professionals can be expected to gather the type of buyer-specific information that's needed to write a good sales proposal, they may need to learn how to sell consultatively.

Question #2: Do your company's sales professionals incorporate the buyer-information gathering that's needed to develop a sales proposal into the selling process?

If your sales professionals are selling consultatively (you answered "Yes" to question #1), it's most likely that they already gather and process lots of buyer-specific information. Much of this information is probably the same information that's needed to write buyer-focused proposals. Remember, this is *process connections information* (PCI) the concept I discussed in Chapter 2.

If your sales professionals aren't selling consultatively (you answered "No" to question #1), it's still possible that they are gathering some buyer-specific information. In other words, your sales professionals may be gathering some of the PCI needed to develop proposals, but, there are probably some PCI gaps that you need to identify.

Whether your sales professionals are selling consultatively or just selling, you need to make sure that the PCI required to develop a proposal is readily available when needed to write the proposal. The information should not just reside in the sales professionals' heads or be buried in their notes. Here's where a thorough understanding of the PCI that goes into a sales proposal is critical.

Question #3: Does your company's senior management understand what it will take to integrate a consultative sales process with a proposal development process?

If your company's senior management wants its sales professionals to sell consultatively and write winning proposals, then senior management may be waiting for someone to tell them what needs to be done, how long it's going to take, and how much it's going to cost. Sounds like a project in the making, but keep reading—you'll get some help.

If your company's senior management doesn't understand what it will take to integrate the processes, you need to sell them on the concepts, guidelines, and ideas in this book. This chapter might give you some ideas.

The Proposal—the Biggest PCI User

In the first two chapters, I stated that selling consultatively is an important ingredient for developing winning, buyer-focused sales proposals. As a sales professional works with the buyer, he must identify and define the *process connections information* (PCI) that will go into a sales proposal. It's important to remember that:

- A sales proposal represents the single biggest user of PCI.

- Many of the activities used to gather the PCI needed in the proposal development process are common with the activities and processes in a consultative sales process—*common activities*.

Sales proposal models, an 80/20 rule, and PCI

Most sales proposal models, for a specific product or service, follow an 80/20 rule: 80 percent of the wording in the proposals is the same for most customers; the remaining 20 percent is buyer specific. As you probably know, much of the 20 percent also represents PCI. This means you can design proposal models, which contain the 80 percent, and provide sales tools for your sales professionals to gather or define the remaining 20 percent. When a sales professional uses a proposal model that contains the 80 percent and adds the 20 percent, the result is a *custom*, buyer-specific proposal.

It's important to note that depending on the subject matter, your proposals might follow 85/15, 75/25, or 90/10 splits. Also, you will probably need to design a proposal model for each product and service that you sell.

Sales tools and PCI

Figure 14-1 is an extract of a large matrix from our book *Why Johnny Can't Sell ...and What to Do About It.* The full matrix shows the interrelationships and timing of sales process phases, sales tools, and process connections information. This matrix only shows some examples of the sales tools that are PCI sources (S) and if that PCI is used (U) in a sales proposal and other sales tools.

Think about the activities one of your sales professional must complete to gather or define the PCI needed in one of your *new* sales proposals. Obviously, some of these sales tools and activities are common to consultative selling and developing sales proposals. But, even if your sales professionals aren't following a consultative sales process, they're probably doing some of the activities needed to develop buyer-focused proposals and they may be using some of the sales tools.

For example, a sales professional might use a "Buyer Questionnaire" to collect specific PCI. The PCI contained in the questionnaire represents required content for the sales proposal and also required information gathered while selling consultatively. Use complete Figure 14-2 as an exercise to help identify:

- Sales tools your sales professionals should use (or will need to use) to gather the PCI used in your *new* sales proposals
- PCI categories in your *new* sales proposals

Figure 14-1 Sources of PCI Used in a Sales Proposal

Sales Tools	Process Connections Information									
	Background Information	Critical Business Issues, KPIs	Impacts on Business	Customer Stated Needs	Customer's Selection Criteria	Product/Service Application	Prices/Fees	Non-Financial Benefits	Financial Benefits	Implementation/ Installation Variables
Customer Intelligence	S	S								
Customer's Web Site	S	S								
Prospect Survey	S	S		S	S					
Buyer Questionnaire	S	S	S	S	S					
KPI Input (Key Pain Indicator)	U	S		S						
Pricing/Configure System		U		U		S	S			S
ROI Valuation	U	S	S	S		U	U		S	
Sales Process Letters (various)	U	U	U	U	U	U	U	S	U	U
Sales Proposal	U	U	U	U	U	U	U	U	U	U

Figure 14-2 Exercise: Sources and Uses of PCI

	Process Connections Information									
Sales Tools										
Sales Proposal	U	U	U	U	U	U	U	U	U	U

Developing Proposal Models

Before your company can get up to speed, it probably needs to develop a new proposal for each product it sells. Often this represents a significant effort, so you might want to establish a project team to participate. Recruit team members from departments that have direct involvement in the proposals' content, such as sales, marketing, product development, and professional services. You might want the completed proposals to follow the five-part structure that I detail in Chapters 4 to 11 of this book.

You should follow these steps to develop and test your new sales proposals:

1. Establish the proposal project team.

2. Define the project goals.

3. Develop an outline for each proposal.

4. Use the outlines to write and approve the proposal or proposals.

5. Test the approved proposals by using them to develop a custom proposal for an actual client.

6. Review the results and make adjustments as needed.

Reverse engineer proposal models

To develop proposal *models*, use the completed custom sales proposals from point 6 above as the starting point. You're going to start with the real customer proposals to reverse engineer your sales proposal *models*. As part of this process, you're most likely going to identify some of the sales tools needed to gather the variable buyer information.

Follow these steps using each new proposal to develop a proposal model(s):

1. Go through each section of the proposal to identify the standard wording, the 80 percent and the buyer variables, the 20 percent. Identify the 20 percent with a highlighter or by underlining the information. The buyer variables represent most of the PCI and are the parts of a proposal that will change from one buyer to the next.

2. On a blank sheet of paper, create a three-column table with four or five rows on each page. Label the columns as follows:

   Sales Tool (source) | **Available (Yes or No)** | **Buyer information**

3. Starting at the beginning of each proposal, follow these steps:
   - Decide and capture the source of each piece of buyer-specific information on a line of your table (sources often are sales tools).
   - Indicate if the Sales Tool is available, Yes or No.
   - List the buyer variable in the sales proposal that uses the sales tool as its source.
   - When you're done, you should have a list that contains the sales tools your sales professionals will use to gather the buyer variables in for each of your sales proposals.

4. Next, turn the completed proposals into a proposal *model* by deleting the actual buyer variable information. Doing so leaves some spaces and blank lines. Keep in mind that the buyer information that sales professionals gather with the sales tools will find a home in one of these spaces or blank lines in the proposal models.

5. Finally, create instructions for your sales professionals that explain which sales tools to use and how to fill in the blanks of each proposal model to develop custom proposals.

When you're done, you will have defined your new proposal models, the supporting sales tools, and the actual document production activities of your proposal development process.

Most sales proposal production systems use some form of the *proposal model* concept to automate production. These automated systems prompt sales professionals to enter buyer-specific information (PCI), the 20 percent, and perhaps select appropriate content from the 80 percent to generate a custom proposal.

Defining Your Proposal Development Process

A process is a particular method of doing something, generally involving a number of activities or operations. Therefore, your company's proposal development process represents:

- Your unique method used by one of your sales professionals to generate a custom sales proposal for a prospective buyer using one of your sales proposal models

- The clearly defined activities or operations your sales professionals follow including the use of various sales tools to gather the buyer information (PCI) required for the proposal

In other words, generating a proposal for your company is no longer an isolated proposal writing activity. Rather, it represents a deliverable from clearly defined set of process activities. Further, proposal development activities often occur over a period of weeks or months rather than during a proposal writing session (or cutting and pasting session) that lasts just a few intense hours or days.

Include post-production activities

You might want to include some post-production activities in your proposal development process. These would represent activities your sales professional might follow to present and deliver the completed proposal to the buyer. Some activities to consider include:

- Reviewing a first draft of the proposal with the contact at the buying organization

- Physically delivering and presenting the completed proposal to the buyer

- Analyzing the results—win-loss analysis perhaps using a sales tool

Use sales tools to help define process activities

Some of the buyer information (or PCI) requirements of your sales proposals might only be met through the use of your sales tools. For example, your sales professionals might use a buyer survey (or questionnaire) to define a buyer's critical business issues and needs. Therefore, the use of a buyer survey represents a required activity of your proposal development process.

While the use of a sales tool can represent a defined activity in your proposal development process, the tool itself might trigger other required process activities. For example, your process might specify the use of a Key Pain Indicator (KPI) input form for an ROI (return on investment) valuation tool. Use of the KPI input form also might trigger the sales professional to write a letter to the buyer that confirms the KPIs identified. Writing the confirmation letter represents another sales proposal development activity that ensures the sales professional doesn't include inaccurate KPIs in his proposal.

Table 14-1 shows how you might define sales tools and activities required for your proposal development process. The sales proposal development phases, activities, sales tools, and PCI categories in Table 14-1 look a lot like those in a consultative sales process because many are the same. I've been discussing the integration of the consultative sales and proposal development process throughout this book. Therefore, Table 14-1 helps identify some of the *common activities* for the two processes.

Perhaps some sales professionals could be successful by simply completing the activities in a proposal development process without a following a sales process. However, I don't recommend that course of action because a consultative selling methodology incorporates questioning techniques, skills, activities, and sales tools not presented in the following table. Rather, as you have read several times in this book, I advocate integrating the two processes. But, sales professionals need to understand that there are two integrated processes. They also need to understand that the process share some *common activities*. Equally important, sales professionals need to recognize that each process has some unique and required activities and sales tools.

Table 14-1 Example Sales Proposal Development Process

Phase	Activities	Sales Tools	PCI Categories
Qualify	• Qualify prospect	• Customer intelligence • Customer's Web site • Confirmation letter or e-mail	• Background • KPIs
Evaluate	• Analyze current situation	• Buyer survey • KPI input • Confirmation letter or e-mail	• Business issues and impacts • Needs
Present	• Configure application • Calculate ROI • Define value proposition	• Pricing/ configuration system • ROI valuation tool • Confirmation letter or e-mail	• Product application • Prices/fees • Non-financial benefits • Financial benefits
Propose	• Develop custom proposal • Internal proposal review and approval • Develop custom presentation and present proposal	• Sales proposal models • Sales proposal production system • Presentation model • Presentation system	• All of above
Due Diligence	• Answer buyer questions • Clarify proposal • Negotiate contracts	• Process letters	• All of above
Close	• Sign contracts • Analyze results	• Win-loss analysis	• n/a

Define proposal systems requirements and production procedures

Don't expect spectacular results if you simply distribute your proposal models as word-processing files and tell the sales professionals to start using them. Rather, define what systems, processes, and procedures the company and its sales professionals need to use to generate a custom proposal using the models.

Consider what word-processing, printing, and binding systems will be needed to produce a sales proposal that reflects your company's quality standards. Develop production procedures that make it easy for sales professionals to generate a proposal. If your sales force is geographically dispersed, you might consider making arranges with an organization that has printing and binding resources nationwide.

Develop performance measurements

Your company, especially its sales managers, needs to monitor the results of the integrated processes. They may find that the *proposal close ratio* (PCR) is an easy and effective way to evaluate individual and group performance and process effectiveness. To monitor results, you need to create a system to measure the success of your sales proposals. Your company must track the result of every proposal that gets written because they can have only one of four outcomes:

- **Won.** The buyer accepted the sales proposal.

- **Lost.** The buyer rejected the sales proposal and selected one of your competitor's sales proposals instead.

- **Pending.** The buyer received the sales proposal but its decision is pending. In other words, your sales proposal is in the buyer's hands but it hasn't made a decision.

- **Abandoned.** The buyer didn't reject your sales proposal and accept a sales proposal from a competitor. Instead, the buyer simply decided not to do anything. For whatever reason, it abandoned any plans to resolve the critical business issues defined in your proposal.

Calculate the proposal close ratio (PCR)

You calculate an individual's, a branch office's, a region's, or your entire company's proposal close ratio (PCR) as follows:

Number of proposals closed ÷ total number of proposals written =
proposal close ratio

Evaluate the impact of an improved PCR

Creating custom sales proposal models for your sales force will increase individual and overall PCRs. This is not rocket science. Giving sales professionals proposal models that require them to sell consultatively to generate quality, buyer-focused sales proposals logically improves results. Answer these questions:

- What's the current PCR for your company?

- How much incremental revenue would your company generate for each percentage point increase in PCR?

- How much does your company need to increase its PCR to justify the investment needed to improve its sales proposal development process?

A high PCR, 50 percent or higher, can mean your company's sales proposals are very effective. Your work creating proposal models and a custom process paid off. However, a very high PCR, 80 percent or higher, might mean that your company's sales professionals are only generating sales proposals for those prospects whom they feel are very likely to buy your company's products. Another possibility is that they're not counting all of their sales proposals in the measurement.

On the other end of the scale, a low PCR (20 percent or lower) can indicate:

- A problem with your sales proposals or the integrated processes. You may need to reevaluate everything.

- The sales professionals are writing too many proposals. Some sales professionals may use the new sales proposals as a crutch. They generate lots of proposals whether the buyers are ready to receive them or not—they try to use the new proposal models to make up for shortcomings or shortcuts in their sales activities.

- Sales professionals are generating proposals with minimal or sketchy buyer information. They're not gathering the required buyer information needed to transform a sales proposal model into a custom, buyer-focused sales proposal.

Your company may want to calculate a PCR for each sales professional. This can make it easy to spot the winners and underachievers. Perhaps the underachievers just need some more help.

Should You Automate Proposal Production?

After everyone in the company realizes that the new proposal models really work, the next thing they might want to do is to automate the proposal *production*. Automating proposal production means your company acquires or develops a system that generates custom sales proposals based upon the input of buyer-specific information.

Without automation, you need to have several tools, procedures, and systems in place:

- Proposal models (usually in the form of a word processing file)

- Sales tools that are sources of the buyer-specific information (mostly PCI) that will be added to the proposal models

- Procedures and instructions for adding the buyer information to the proposal models

- A word-processing system that the sales professionals use to store and access the proposal models, insert the buyer information, and print custom proposals

An automated proposal production system allows sales professionals to insert buyer information into the proper places in a proposal model and then generate a custom proposal. Some automated systems present sales professionals with questions to expedite process. These systems then output generated proposals in word-processing system format.

Note: You will still need some sales tools even with an automated production process—these sales tools represent the sources (S) of PCI needed in a proposal.

Decide if your company is an automation candidate

Before you go ahead with automation, evaluate whether your company is a good candidate. Use the criteria in Table 14-2 to help you decide.

Table 14-2 Proposal Automation Criteria

Criteria	Considerations
Number of sales professionals	If your company employs many sales professionals, automating the production process makes sense; cost-justifying automation is easier when many people benefit.
Geographic dispersal	If your company's sales professionals are spread out all over the country, automating sales proposal production helps insure content consistency.
Proposal production time and cost	Calculate how long it takes and how much it costs to write a proposal without an automated production system. If a sales professional has to spend 4 to 5 hours writing a sales proposal, that's costly. Further, the sales professional's time would be better spent selling.
Number of products sold	If your company needs proposal models for many products, automating proposal production makes maintaining and controlling the proposal models easier. Sales professionals will have only one source for the models: the automated proposal production system.
Frequent changes to product offerings	If your company frequently makes changes to its product offerings, then automating production helps ensure that sales professionals use the most current version of a proposal model.

Benefits for Automating Proposal Production

Automating proposal production in your company provides non-financial and financial benefits.

Identify non-financial benefits

Table 14-3 presents some of the features that you can expect to have in an automated proposal system and the resulting non-financial benefits.

Table 14-3 Non-Financial Benefits of Automation

Feature	Benefits
Proposal model database	• Ensures quality, consistency, and corporate branding for all proposals • Allows sales professionals to select the correct model from a proposal database • Allows rapid deployment and easy updating so everyone has access to the most current proposal versions
Online input of buyer-specific information	• Provides easy input by sales professionals of buyer-specific information on formatted input screens either to an Internet- or Intranet-based, standalone PC, or server system • Optionally, interfaces with the company's contact management or customer relationship management system, which may contain some of the buyer-specific information fields needed to generate a custom sales proposal
Proposals generated in word-processing system format	• Generates perfectly formatted proposals—no cutting and pasting and no time wasted trying to correct formatting problems • Allows sales professionals easily to edit generated proposals
Activity and management reporting	• Provides sales professionals and management with proposal activity and status reporting • Provides sales professionals and management with access to the PCR for the company, division, and individual

Calculate financial benefits of automation

Calculate the financial benefits of automating proposal production by comparing current, manual production costs and times to those of the automated system. Use these key pain indicators:

- **Number of Proposals** written annually

- **Average Time**, in hours, needed to write a custom proposal

- **Cost** of a sales professional to write proposals. You can include one of two costs in your calculation:

  - **Opportunity Cost** (hourly) = Average Annual Quota of a sales professional ÷ 2,000 hours in a year

  - **Fully-Loaded Cost** (hourly) = Average Salary + Benefits of a sales professional ÷ 2,000 hours in a year

Use these key pain indicators to calculate the cost to write and produce one proposal using the current manual process.

- **Cost to Produce a Proposal** = Average Time x Opportunity Cost or Average Time x Fully-Loaded Cost

- **Annual Proposal Production Costs** = Number of Proposals x Cost to Product a Proposal

Calculate the total cost to produce one proposal using these key pain indicators:

- **Total Annual Automated System Cost**. If you plan to:

  - Use software as a service (SaaS), this can include but is not limited to: all total annual costs of the service.

  - License an existing system, this can include but is not limited to: one-year's amortized cost, annual cost of funds, software maintenance, and internal equipment and support costs.

  - Design and develop a system, this can include but is not limited to: one-year's amortized development costs, cost of funds, and internal equipment and support costs.

- **Cost to Produce a Proposal** using the automated system = Total Annual Automated System Cost ÷ Number of Proposals

Calculate the financial benefits for automating proposal production by comparing total annual production costs and costs to produce one proposal. Of course, these cost comparisons include the reduced production time experienced by the sales force.

Stuff to Remember

Johnny and his team were finally done. They all believed that they had achieved Johnny's goal to design and develop the best proposals in the industry. Along the way they had gained tremendous insight into what buyers expect to see in a seller's sales proposal. They also received unexpected and enthusiastic support from several others within the company. Their new sales proposal development process added the discipline that was lacking in their sales process. All they had to do now was execute!

Johnny decided he would closely monitor results. He set up a spreadsheet to keep track of proposal activity for each team member. He planned to monitor production activity and to calculate individual and collective proposal close ratios. Based on Johnny's preliminary calculations, he thought he was very close to cost-justifying an automated proposal production system. He just needed a bit more revenue and a few more team members—that seemed very attainable.

√ Most sales proposal models follow an 80/20 rule: 80 percent of the wording in sales proposals is the same for most customers; the remaining 20 percent is buyer-specific.

√ Use a live, completed sales proposal as the starting point to reverse engineer a sales proposal model and perhaps some of the sales tools needed to gather the required buyer information.

√ Include the systems and production procedures needed to generate a proposal in your proposal development process.

√ You want to include some post-production activities in your proposal development process—activities your sales professional might follow to present and deliver the completed proposal to the buyer.

√ To monitor results, your company needs to calculate proposal close ratios.

√ Your company might want to automate the proposal production, in which an automated proposal production system allows sales professionals to insert buyer information into the proper places in a proposal model to generate a custom proposal.

√ Automating proposal production can provide significant non-financial and financial benefits.

Resources

www.salesproposals.com

This is our company's Web site. You'll find information about our:

- Services
- Sales Document Builder, our Web-based sales proposal and document production system
- Partners

Our site also contains a "Resources" page.

www.whyjohnnycantsell.com

The "Resource" page on this site contains:

- Recommended books
- Sources for several categories of sales-related systems, consultants, tools, and products